31-day transformational challenge guide

THE NEW MOVE...

The Chronicles Of Living A Spirit Life!

By Olga H. Matsanura

Printed in Cyprus by Deep Insight Publishing House

THE NEW MOVE...

31-day transformational challenge guide

Contents

Introduction

Expect true transformation and enlightenment through this 31-day journey to studying, reading and replicating the Word of God to find expression through you. This journey you are about to embark on will help you regain your spiritual immunity through the simple concepts in the daily and timely word. Be open-hearted and willing to receive in order to communicate the Spirit kind of life. We have been made able ministers of the Spirit and that same Spirit giveth life. This challenge simply guides you to learn to come to the fullness and full confidence of who you are as a son of God and the assurance of the dominion, power, influence, value and authority you carry and host as a spirit being. There is a kind of strength and stability your soul captures when you discover the purpose of your existence and the divine mandate. It is that time for the new move of true born-again sons to cultivate awareness, practice and demonstrate the constant presence of God, developing spiritual habits and discipline that many can boldly look up to and see the glory and glorify the Father. Our sole duty is to be the exact representation of the manifestation of the expression of God and the kingdom come to be seen in us in this season of the new move. Many are complaining about the world system, the gross darkness filling the people, but I am here to announce to you that you have what it takes; the capacity and ability, the conviction and confirmation, the love and affection, the faith and the Word to shine forth your light; for kings to come to the brightness of thy rising, to give flavor to the cosmos, to give color to your generation and to show forth your peculiarity. Time for prolonging your destiny is over; the season of being a generational thief is over. *"ARISE, shine; for thy light is come, and the glory of the LORD is risen upon thee."*

Isaiah 60:1 (KJV).

I pray this thirty one-day challenge transforms your inner man and your soul and that the Spirit ministers to you expressly beyond just the written word. May the grace to act on the Word be released to you and for the Word to be tangible to you. Let mercy speak on your behalf in Jesus' Name. Enjoy the cruise; it is worth it, and I await your testimonies!

A Prayer, To Be Saved, And Be Born-Again

Suppose you are not born again and desire to receive Christ and a fresh baptism of the Holy Ghost. If you are willing and genuinely saying, I want the Lord to be my savior and receive salvation. This is your moment to receive the very life and nature of God into your heart. It is an act of faith receiving Christ into your spirit. He will perfect His will in your life. Distance is not a barrier; it is not about proximity; it is about the genuineness of your heart!

Say this short prayer;

Oh Lord God, my Father, my Maker. I believe with all my heart in Jesus Christ, the Son of God. I believe He died for me. I believe God raised Him from the dead, and He is alive today. And by my faith in Jesus Christ, I receive Him as Lord of my life. I confess the Lordship of Jesus Christ over my life, and I receive eternal life into my heart and my spirit. Thank you, Lord, for saving my soul. I have eternal life now by my faith in Jesus Christ. Thank you, Lord, for giving me a new life, and I pray now that you will keep my heart fixed on you. From today I am hidden with Christ in God. Thank you, Father, for the gift of salvation in Jesus' Name.

Amen

A holistic body in Christ

We are a mystical body that should be grounded in a profoundly realistic manner, in union with God and in unity with each other to mirror the fulness of the Godhead.

DAY 1

And Jesus knew their thoughts, and said unto them, Every kingdom divided against itself is brought to desolation; and every city or house divided against itself shall not stand.
Matthew 12: 25 (KJV)

As sons of God that we are, we are from the kingdom of God. We are not called to pull down or destroy others in the kingdom. It is against our constitution and testament. We often discredit and envy one another's gifts, talents, grace, anointing, favor, influence and power at work in their lives. This should not be so amongst us; remember, a kingdom and a house divided against itself cannot stand! We easily forget that it is the same Father that hides those gifts in them, and it is because of their quest of discovering and exercising by reason of use that has made them manifest and fully express that which we envy and despise. What manner of ignorance that has befallen amongst our fellow brethren of going against the very scriptures we proclaim; *"For as we have many members in one body, and all members have not the same office: So; we, being many, are one body in Christ, and every one members one of another. Having then gifts differing according to the grace that is given to us…"* Romans 12:5 (KJV).

We limit the ability, capacity, vast possibilities and provisions of God when we pull, destroy and kill others' gifts entrusted to them. Learn to appreciate the dimension of the manifestation of God upon those that have gone ahead of you and those that have what you desire. We are all one body with different functional parts that work collectively, holistically as a body in Christ.

How can you be a partaker of that which you despise? How can you desire to have the same access when your track record in the Spirit is fighting against you and saying otherwise? Let us, therefore, be wise. *"See then that ye walk circumspectly, not as fools, but as wise." Ephesians 5:15 (KJV).* Learn to celebrate one another, honor one another's gifts and rejoice in the expression of a dimension of God in their lives. It is amazing, sweet and great when you are in possession of such great gifts and yet bemusing when not received and rejected by you; and when you are not privileged to be the host of that kind of dimension of God! *"And let us consider [thoughtfully] how we may encourage one another to love and to do good deeds, not forsaking our meeting together [as believers for worship and instruction], as is the habit of some, but encouraging one another; and all the more [faithfully] as you see the day [of Christ's return] approaching." Hebrews 10:24-25 (AMP).* Do not allow yourself to be a material, an agent used by the enemy for destruction. Help build others and encourage them. God will give you endurance and encouragement to give others and the same attitude of mind towards each other. God has given us spiritual gifts to make us strong and that we may be mutually encouraged by each other's faith. We have been blessed with all spiritual blessings in heavenly places in Christ. Let us put on a new self and put away our old ways and see God trust us with His fullness of the Godhead bodily dwelling in us. The effective use of your life, gifts and resources to draw men to Jesus makes you become a blessing to humanity.

If you are procrastinating on acting on the Word, then you need to re-read the passage again for the day; with repentance. The Word is alive and active when it is spoken from the right place!

Here's something you should carry with you today: Appreciation is key to walking in the divinity, glory, grace, authority, anointing, power of influence, and to express the same move of God in your life. You can never receive and enjoy the full benefits of what you do not honor in the kingdom!

Declaration

Father in the Name of Jesus, I thank you for this timely word that has brought light into my spirit. I declare that from today, I walk circumspectly as wise in the true transformation of your Word. I repent from pulling down and insulting my brother, my sister of that which you have sent them for the edification of the body of Christ. For every action that I might have done in the past to divide your kingdom, Lord, from today, I repent and ask for your forgiveness from any curse that I might have brought to myself. Father from today, I find my role in the body of Christ and I play it with all my heart. I will learn from today to walk in love and appreciate your dimension's expression and manifestation in others' lives. Thank you, Abba Father, for I know you have heard me, and from today I enjoy the full benefits of the kingdom because I have been set free and free; indeed I am!

Alignment and keying into the new move

Our reception level to align to what God wants to do in us and through us guarantees spiritual illumination to be set apart from the ordinary!

02

DAY 2

And be not conformed to this world [any longer with its superficial values and customs], but be transformed and progressively changed [as you mature spiritually] by the renewing of your mind [focusing on Godly values and ethical attitudes], so that you may prove [for yourselves] what the will of God is, that which is good and acceptable and perfect [in His plan and purpose foryou].

Romans 12:2 (AMP)

The world is rapidly changing tremendously. Its system is transforming right before our eyes. The propensity and dissemination of social media have colonized many activities. Very soon, most of our needs and wants would have transcended. If not, they have already transcended to the digital platform and taken facets of dispensation.

On the other hand, there's a new move in the realms of the Spirit that requires those that are sensitive, deliberate, diligent and committed to God and growth to stand in this era. This is no time to be frivolous, rather be grounded to the embassy of the kingdom. Many may be carried away and conform to this world's pattern and will miss the agenda of God. This is a season of the new move of breaking and disconnecting from the mindset that establishes itself as leverage in your life. Be conscious and yielded in this season. Do not let anything have you that is not of God.

Unfortunately, many do not want to hear this; but we are in the last days [perilous times]. The days that only those that know their God shall be strong and shall draw strength from the knowledge and revelation that has entered, and that is in contact with their spirit. The logos, the Word, makes us understand; *"This know also, that in the last days perilous times shall come." 1 Timothy 3:1 (KJV).* Be careful not to follow different kinds of smoke [worldly trends] and be swallowed by this world's system and not shine. Use this precious gift that is time to align yourself to God's will so that the world will not dictate your life. Remember, the unit of your destiny is time and whatsoever that affects your time affects your destiny. If you yield yourself to worldly trends, then you will become a student of it. Whatever you yield yourself to, you will become a student of it.

Align yourself to kingdom come. *"And it shall come to pass in the last days, saith God, I will pour out my Spirit upon all flesh: and your sons and your daughters shall prophesy, and your young men shall see visions, and your old men shall see dreams." Acts 2:17 (KJV).* This is surely your portion. This is a new era; we must be spiritually equipped with the word of God so as not to be swallowed by the devious system of this world and lose our relevance. This is a season we must seek God beyond the confinements of a church building. It is that time we should invest in spiritual development. A generation that knows its identity walks in power! Let us, therefore, be sincere with God. Let us hunger for more to grow spiritually and defeat the agenda of the enemy. Your hunger will attract a dimension of God and encounters. Sons of God let us subscribe to the principles of the kingdom.

You are more than a conqueror, and you will prevail if you stay true and connected to His word that is ye and amen. Wear your crown, wear your sonship, wear your priesthood and overcome!

Here's something you should carry with you today: God already knows those that are His, and you have been chosen right from the beginning of eternity. You are the chosen generation, a royal priesthood, a holy nation called to show forth your peculiarity and bring about the change this world is crying for. You have been separated from darkness into His marvelous light. Shine forth, and I say, go ye into this world and shine!

Declaration

Father, I come boldly to your throne of grace that I may obtain mercy and find grace to help in time of need. Lord help me in this season not to conform to the pattern of this world. I declare, and I decree that I am a citizen, an ambassador, a replica and a representative of the kingdom embassy. My life is not dictated and dependent on the embassy of this world. I arise, and I shine. I am committed, dedicated, deliberate and diligent in the process of growth. I wear the mentality mindset of a leader; I wear my identity as a son, a king, a priest and as a God! I am spiritually equipped, spiritually sound, spiritually civilized and spiritually literate in the Word. Lord, as the world is advancing in its technology, Father, I advance in the knowledge of your Will and your kingdom. My mind is renewed and washed daily with your Word. I nurture the Word inside me to see the fullness and establishment of your purpose over my life. I flourish this season in the Name of Jesus.

Thank you, Father, for being my guide and for Your Word that is a lamp unto my feet and a light unto my path.

Knowing your role, you have to play for the kingdom to eradicate ignorance and disobedience

It is important to know the reality of the Christ in you that makes for divinity to find expression in you!

DAY 3

As obedient children, not fashioning yourselves according to the former lusts in your ignorance:

1 Peter 1:14 (KJV)

For by the grace [of God] given to me I say to everyone of you not to think more highly of himself [and of his importance and ability] than he ought to think; but to think so as to have sound judgement, as God has apportioned to each a degree of faith [and a purpose designed for service].

Romans 12:3 (AMP)

He who learns from instruction and correction is on the [right] path of life [and for others his example is a path toward wisdom and blessing], But he who ignores and refuses correction goes off course [and for others his example is a path toward sin and ruin].

Proverbs 10:17 (AMP)

Making oneself available for the Master's use, diligently, deliberately, consistently, with commitment and dedication, being disciplined as a sacrifice; sets you up for abundance! I once came across a man of God teaching on obedience: He mentioned that obedience equates to abundance only if you are obedient to allow God to use you expressly. If you love God, you will obey His will. "If ye be willing and obedient, ye shall eat the good of the land:" Isaiah 1:19 (KJV). Your eating of the good of the land is tied to your obedience. God will do wonders in your life when you are obedient to His instruction and His will for you over your life. It is surely a guaranteed and a chivalrous reward that calls upon the ministry of your ministering spirits sent for you and consecration of your desires to fulfillment. Learn to take heed to an instruction from the Spirit; do not think more highly of yourself. We are all called to serve Him. Have the mindset of a server.

It is imperative to allow yourself to be used by God for His glory and His kingdom to be expressed and come through you. You have a role to play in the kingdom, and you have to play it with all your heart. Do not let anything steal this moment from you by any means. God wants to give you a mantle that supersedes your age. Your availability and obedience to the voice of the Spirit will make you become a host of the exact representation of the extension of the character of Jesus Christ. This is a season where God is using those that desire to be used genuinely.

The question you may want to ask yourself is: *Am I ready, and do I want to be used to show forth His glory and be a representative of the carrier of the kingdom manifestations?* God wants to begin with you. Yes, you that is reading this devotional! You are already anointed; the anointing is the experience of God meant for you to activate and perform. The anointing you carry is calling you to the assignment of God that will set you apart. God rewards on how faithful you are and how disciplined and obedient you are willing to be wasted by Him. Your investment in your hunger will determine your placement in the new move and on the agenda of God. This is a new season for our generation to experience God evidentially, undeniably and unapologetically. Taking advantage and keying to the move and the season is important for your relevance. You cannot afford to be irrelevant [operating outside the jurisdiction of the Will of the Father] in this world. Let Christianity not be a mockery where many question the powerlessness of sons of God and your sonship. Take away prayerlessness and worldliness from your hearts. Do not be deceived by what is going on around the world. Use this time to cook yourself; there's so much you can do for the kingdom according to the measure of your faith, the grace and the functioning of your faith. Engage your faith and begin to enjoy the benefits of your faith! Make yourself available; this can take you far in life, especially now that there are no distractions; you can revive your secret place effectively. This is my heart cry to you.

Here's something you should carry with you today: God is looking for willing vessels of honor that will serve in His government and bring heaven here on earth and manifest the kingdom that is to come. Be a part if you can and if you will.

Declaration

Lord Jesus, help me to be obedient to your Will and instructions. I refuse this day, Lord, to exalt myself and think highly of myself. I want to be wasted by you. I want to obey you and eat the good of the land. I make myself available for use, and I devote myself diligently, deliberately, with dedication and discipline. I offer myself as a sacrifice. Make me holy and acceptable to you, Lord. I hunger for more of you. Consecrate me, Lord. I develop and cultivate the mindset of a server and the workmanship of my Father's government. I align myself to the kingdom come. Let nothing steal this moment from me. I am an embodiment of the nature and character of Christ. I am a carrier of the kingdom manifestations. I stand as a representative that progresses the kingdom. I take advantage, and I key into the season. I am heavenly defended and backed by the Spirit.

Thank you, Father, for choosing me to be a partaker of your divine glory.

Walking circumspectly to accomplish success in all ramifications

It is a requirement to be wise in the kingdom; being prayerful to yield to the process of building, in order not to be limited and to perceive through the lens of misfortunes and needs only.

DAY 4

See then that ye walk circumspectly, not as fools, but as wise.

Ephesians 5:15 (KJV)

But seek ye first the kingdom of God, and his righteousness; and all these things shall be added unto you.

Matthew 6:33 (KJV)

We are often seeking to be great, wealthy, successful, influential, powerful, exhibit value, and be the most anointed amongst them all. Success is an accomplishment of worthy goals. Take note I said worthy goals. It is not just the ability to show forth what you have achieved or accomplished. It is also who you are becoming. Anything achieved outside of God does not count in the kingdom. It is irrelevant. Your wealth creation starts from the mind of Christ and not in the outcome. You become loaded with worldly possessions physically and be an empty brass spiritually. We often are oppressed, frustrated, bemused, offended and vexed when we see the ease in others' lives versus our frustration and lack of results in our lives. The truth is some people will never forgive; they will always envy, despise you and will always be offended at you for being ahead of them in life. It is your progress they cannot tolerate, your blessings they cannot match, and your favor they cannot stand! You are anointed, the anointing is the experience of God, and you have been given access to activate and perform.

Some may try to blame God for their misfortunes and afflictions. For how long will you continue in this ignorance, in this spiritual illiteracy? Let us walk circumspectly as wise. I have been a victim for so long, and I have allowed the process of healing and time to transform me and to find expression through me. Do not deceive yourself and build on a faulty foundation. Build on the Word that is sure to yield you proceeds that remain. Remember, you define your future by the extent of your transformation [light], and you can attract His will [knowledge]. I am not motivating you: I am trying to bring you into a dimension and realization of who God wants you to be. It is time to wake up, to arise and know your identity as a believer. No more excuses! Allow virtue to find expression through you- the character of Christ in you. Allow God to be fully expressed in you. His Godhead bodily must dwell in you. Keep pressing through desire and hunger and see protocols being broken for your sake. Allow the consciousness and yieldedness of your heart, mind and spirit to intercourse and reveal the nature and character of God.

The secret is seeking first the kingdom. Surprisingly, it is possible for you to know the degree to which the kingdom has come in you. When you have managed to sustain and develop God's atmosphere, your prayer will be more on kingdom advancement, creating a healthy prayer life. When your prayer increases in your needs' consciousness, then the kingdom has not fully come in you. There is a scarcity of a healthy prayer life. Your Father is aware of your needs, and once you seek the kingdom, things will start attracting and attaching themselves to you. It is easier to command things in the realm of the spirit and for material things to attach themselves to you when you are aligned to His will and seeking Him.

Certain principles are revealed and made known to you as a result of genuine dedication to seeking Him. Your needs are a symptom of the absence of the kingdom's influence and the lack of light and sight in the ability and reality of the endless possibilities of God's expression in your life. The reception level of the kingdom guarantees spiritual illumination. It enables your focus to be shifted from wanting to be; to becoming the exact representation of the character of the Christ that has found expression in you [this is the kingdom]. And all these things will be added unto you and attach themselves to the pattern and the word in contact with your spirit. Do not allow anything to waste and have you that is not of God. Everything you will ever want and need is in Matthew 6:33.

Here's something you should carry with you today: You carry the kingdom. Your prayer pattern should change, knowing that your prayers' primary assignment should align with His will to bring the kingdom its fulfillment. Shift your focus from the needs. It is that time for a defining moment for someone to shift.

Declaration

Heavenly Father, I thank you because I have received your wisdom. I believe, and I speak of the light of the knowledge of your glory. Henceforth, I seek first your kingdom, and I set my eyes on the things above. I receive light, and I receive transformation. I build on the precision of the Word of God. I attract the attention of God, and His Will is finding full expression through me. I attract endless possibilities of God. I command all that I need to attach themselves to me. Thank you, Daddy, for being a good, good Father. You know my needs before I even ask. I develop a relationship that sorely seeks your Person. Today I allow virtue to find expression in me and through me in Jesus' Name.

Thank you, Father, because I know I am enjoying Your dimensions in my dealings and every aspect of my life.

The power of speaking right

There is a healing that must take place in the area of your perception to change in position!

05

DAY 5

Death and life are in the power of the tongue: and they that love it shall eat the fruit thereof.

Proverbs 18:21 (KJV)

It is the spirit that quickeneth; the flesh profiteth nothing: the words that I speak unto you, they are spirit, and they are life.

John 6:63 (KJV)

...for of the abundance of the heart his mouth speaketh.

Luke 6:45 (KJV)

Let no corrupt communication proceed out of your mouth, but that which is good to the use of edifying, that it may minister grace unto hearers.

Ephesians 4:29 (KJV)

The power of speaking may never be overemphasized. That means in your mouth, and your tongue lies the power of life and death. We need to guard our lips for our lives not to be ruined. Learn to use your mouth for a good cause. Do not give the enemy room to temper with your identity and destiny. We all have two prayer warriors in us, which is the mind and our mouth. Create an aura for your prayer warriors to fully express the Christ in you without being choked. A closed mouth is a closed destiny, and a clogged mind is a blocked realm for transportation! Your imagination, especially in this season, is a pacesetter for your destination. Develop confidence in His plan to the extent that you do not even get upset when things do not go your way.

Do you want to manifest the kingdom? Do you want your life to be the exact extension and representation of the kingdom here on earth? You have the resources [your warriors] to act on your behalf. That is why it is very important to be spiritually sound and civilized to connect and collect from the wells of salvation and the rivers of living waters. Keep your warriors from being contaminated by the afflictions, cares and circumstances of this world. Do not let your mind become a battlefield of thoughts not inspired by the Holy Spirit. Gain control over your warriors and find freedom and peace that surpasses all understanding. As a man thinketh in his heart, so is he. The degree and extent to which God finds expression and influence in your life are linked to the way you utter the Word that is in your spirit and measured by your yieldedness to His leading. God gave you a mouth to speak life, the mind to conceive and drive your life in the direction that aligns with His will. Your mind is a forerunner of the actions that your warriors give birth. Correct that spiritual atmosphere to key into the Will of God.

Set your mind on the things above, remember what goes into someone's mouth does not defile him but what comes out of their mouth is what defiles them [thoughts]. Do not allow your mind to develop a cloud that houses the energy that attracts the enemy because you will weaken the aspect of your speaking and your effectiveness. Many have been speaking and still speak, but speaking is when the light comes. That moment you encounter light, you begin to see the light, then you will start to speak the mind of God, to command the earth to answer to you. Do not let anything choke or abort the Word in your spirit that should be uttered to give life. God did not employ a mouthpiece for you and on your behalf; rather, He gave you ministering spirits who act on the Word that aligns with His will. Keep speaking; your speaking is an act of demonstrating your faith [engagement of your faith and the Word] and the dominion mandate you carry. Exercise your mouth until your tongue muscles masters the thought pattern that is in sync with the Word and the mind of God.

Issues we may face are a result of the absence and the abortion of right speaking. It is the absence of your dominion and spiritual ignorance on the authority you possess as a spirit-filled being. Start speaking right and declare what you want to be established. Never allow the devil to dictate what he has no power or influence over. Start speaking words that are constant and confirm the truth [Word]. Your state of mind matters to your terminology. Do not allow the enemy to paralyze your mind and close your mouth from speaking the reality of the Word that must come to pass in your life. Never be intimidated by circumstances in your circumferences to think God has failed you. God is still in the business of making your words come to pass.

Here's something you should carry with you today: There's nothing conceivable by the mind that is not obtainable. Channel and speak into existence your blessings!

Declaration

Father in the Name of Jesus, I declare that from today I set a watch before my mouth and I keep the door of my lips. I am anointed to speak spirit, light and life. From my tongue proceeds, only life, and I refrain from speaking death to my soul. I communicate that which is good and edifies my soul. My tongue is soothing. I set my mind on the things above to know the right words to communicate with my soul. I fully exercise my prayer warriors to bring into manifestation the life I declare upon my circumferences. I refuse to close my destiny because of a closed mouth. I give no room for the enemy to temper with my destiny. I keep my mind right, and I conquer. I exercise my dominion in my speaking. Thank you, Father, because I know I have the mind of Christ. I can never be defeated in the realm of my mind because I take charge! I carry the atmosphere that breeds possibilities.

Thank you, Daddy, for the dominion given to me to exercise.

Yielding to change

Allowing transformation to take place in your life eliminates many problems and unnecessary delays, allowing for those things that belong to you to attach themselves back to you.

DAY 6

For which cause we faint not; but though our outward man perish, yet the inward man is renewed day by day.
2 Corinthians 4:16 (KJV)

Therefore if any man be in Christ, he is a new creature: old things are passed away, behold, all things are become new.
2 Corinthians 5:17 (KJV)

That ye put off concerning the former conversation the old man, which is corrupt according to the deceitful lusts;
Ephesians 4:22 (KJV)

Change is not about perfection. It is the ability and the capacity to move from one place of bondage and stagnation. It is a continuous transformation of making yourself be the best version heaven recognizes. Allow God to purge you from the things that do not identify with Him. You are the righteousness of God in Christ Jesus. Study and take the time to learn about the sons of God manual. Learn about your identity as a believer. Learn about who you are as a person, who you represent, where you are going, where you belong and whose path you belong to. Develop and build confidence. Do not allow anything to have you that is not from God and of God. You do not need a century to effect change; you only need effective preparation to provoke unusual transformations.

As it is, you are a kingdom asset, investment heaven recognizes and is committed to nurturing. In this world, we have many generational thieves that have refused and neglected their relevance and influence by not manifesting that which God has deposited in them to exert dominion over the affairs of their lives. Some of us have robbed our generation of that which must find expression in us and through us. What is in you is not for you; allow change to bring forth the beauty of the character of God in you. What you carry is for nations' manifestation! You cannot afford to translate with all that is hidden inside of you. If you do not run away from that which does not belong to you, that which belongs to you may never come.

We all, at one point, if not constantly, receive prophecies. Yes, the testimony of Jesus is the Spirit of prophecy! But prophecy, in as much as it is a good thing, has pushed you, and your lack of transformation reversed you back and brought you back. You will complain from today till Jesus comes that many of your prophecies did not come to pass because you never fulfilled your part of the bargain. You cannot do different things the same way; rather, you can make changes in a great way that brings greatness to your soul. Change comes from your mind's interaction and the commitment to constant fellowship with the Spirit of God. Until this is in sync, then the atmosphere for change is introduced for transformation. Be connected to the spiritual strength of God for His strength to be made perfect in your weakness. Allow the Holy Spirit to be your mentor and make yourself the mentee in bringing about the change for the kingdom's manifestation in you. Never see yourself as small, change. You are a son of God not by gender but by inheritance. God is interested and committed to you. You cannot change by just believing. Even faith without works is dead. You change by acting towards change as your participatory role. Observe and do; it is never too late to make adjustments in the spirit. Heaven rejoices in your willingness to be involved.

Here's something you should carry with you today: Your assignment is embedded in your diligence to find your participatory role and connect to the truth [Word] that you want to see manifest that is consistent with the character of Christ. Enter into that dimension of conviction and confirmation.

Declaration

Oh, Great God, I thank you for the explosion of your goodness upon my life. Thank you for transforming me into the son you have always intended for me to become. Your Word is true; your Word brings reproach and correction. I receive the ability and capacity to separate myself from stagnation and bondage. I disconnect myself from associations that do not identify with your Will. I am a new creature in Christ Jesus. Old things have passed away. I embrace positive change. I am spiritually inclined. I wear a new garment of the righteousness of God. The old nature in me is aborted in Jesus' Name. I am free, and I refuse to be a generational thief. I am relevant to my generation because I am born of God. I command all that is meant for me to locate me now! I am committed to continuing my process of being transformed by the Word in the Name of Jesus.

Thank you, Lord, for I know my life will never remain stagnant and never will it remain the same. As I have declared in His name, so shall it be!

Awakening the Sons

This is the season for born again believers to arise and shine forth the dimensions of God they carry; the divinity of Christ to find portals for expression in humanity through them.

DAY 7

ARISE, shine, for thy light is come, and the glory of the LORD is risen upon thee. For, behold, the darkness shall cover the earth, and gross darkness the people: but the LORD shall arise upon thee, and his glory shall be seen upon thee. And Gentiles shall come to thy light, and kings to the brightness of thy rising.

Isaiah 60:1-3 (KJV)

The reawakening…
The reawakening. The testament of influence is come!

Sons of God wake up, sons of God wake up. The time for slumber has passed. The time to launch is come and is now. See now, the season to shine is now. The season of identification is now. The days and seasons to be powerless and irrelevant as sons have passed. Nations await your manifestation. *"For the earnest expectation of the creature waiteth for the manifestation of the sons of God." Romans 8:19 (KJV).*
Kings only come to the brightness of thy rising. Arise! Arise! Arise!!!

God's anointing is bestowed upon you. We are in the season of men of encounters. We are the sons that have been entrusted on this earth. As we have experienced God's mentality with our minds, it is time to experience Him with our hearts. We are a citizenry of people that have influence and give expression to the Will of the Father. As sons, our value is on the assignment that can be committed to us in the kingdom. Your assignment is simply your contribution to the world expressing the kingdom. The fulness of your encounter is sustained and demonstrated by the quality of your alignment. This is your time to fully align to the plan, move and wave of God. You have already the empowerment of the Spirit to be impactful. Arise, shine! We are men of spiritual illumination and shekinah glory. Men of encounters are men of power, influence, contribution, value, and dominion: men who never waver. This is a testament to the dominion of the Sons of God. You are a man of experience who manifest the presence of God. It is time for your triumphant entry as Sons. God is looking for those that will put pressure on His integrity and attention. You will attract the attention of God when aligned to the Will of the Father. Your destiny is at the mercy of the dimension of God that you know. All you see is not all there is. It's time to seek for the greater in you than he that is in the world. When God empowers you, understand that no man can pull you down. You are anointed, and that anointing is the experience of God meant for you to activate and to perform. Start praying for the other sons to take up their cross and to position themselves in their respective positions to enter into the dimension of their consciousness. As for you who is reading this, you are a part of the move and the kingdom already; you are part of heaven's government. Yes, you! You are anointed, appointed, an altar; the ecclesia accounted for in the kingdom and the replica of God. Believe it, it is true. Your Father loves you. You carry the atmosphere this generation is longing for. Be the blessing that you are because you are anointed. Align yourself, myself included, to attract God's attention and the kingdom come dimension. Be a kingdom carrier, a host, a representative, an ambassador, a king, an extension of God for the total expression of the fullness of the Godhead to be seen in you and through you.

Allow your color to show. Change your location to align with your allocation in the Spirit. The appointment for your allocation and anointing is now! You have anointing and power that many will debate and be controversial about. Raw power shall be seen in these last days and through you. Do you believe you will be a contributor to the kingdom come? You are loaded, reloaded, and preloaded before the eternity of time! You are the brightness of His glory, the express image of His person. It is time to launch!

Encounters lead to revelation, and by revelation, conviction is birthed and produces faith that leads to obedience. These actions of obedience produce results. Encounters are a dimension of God; you will discover as you go deeper with Him. It is not by age nor by many years of being a Christian. It is about your brokenness. How far you have yielded His Lordship.

Here's something you should carry with you today: Shout and tell destiny that here I come!!

Declaration

Father in the Name of Jesus, I thank you for having called me for such a time and season. I arise to the call to action. I shine forth the glory of my Father. Thank you for your Spirit that is quickening my mortal body. Thank you for the glory that has risen upon me. You have called me to shine forth the light I carry already. Oh, my Father, my Maker, the Father of lights be thou glorified as I shine in this world. I declare, and I know that it is my sole duty and purpose to spread the kingdom abroad. I know I am experiencing the surpassing greatness of your covering and your favor. As I rise, Father, you will not fail me. I align myself to your Will. I am giving birth to the kingdom and the promises of God. I have been equipped, empowered, strengthened, favored and graced. I overcome and impact the world, and I stand as an ambassador of the establishment of the kingdom come. I connect intentionally to this move in the Name of Jesus. I am contributing to the kingdom and my world. I am anointed, and the jealousy of God is invested upon me. I influence and take charge of the affairs of my dealings.

Thank you, Daddy, for I am aligning to the move of the kingdom this season.

Pulling down strongholds and purging unwanted stuff from the shelves of our minds

Emptying oneself from the thoughts that do not conform to the knowledge of our God is important, and creating a pattern and an atmosphere for protecting our minds from being empty so as not to give the devil a pathway for manipulation.

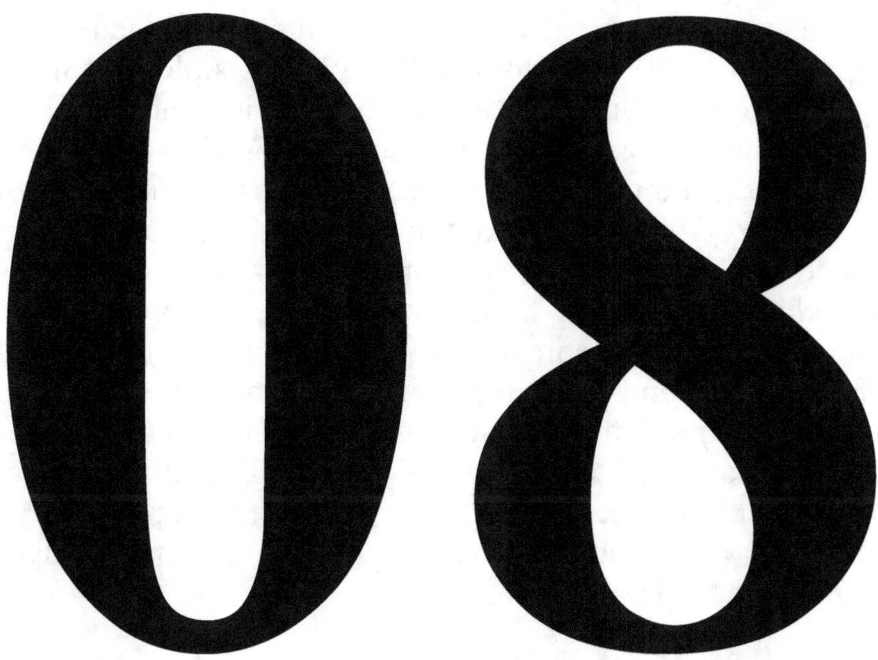

DAY 8

For the weapon of our warfare are not carnal, but mighty through God to the pulling down of strongholds; Casting down imaginations, and every high thing that exalteth itself against the knowledge of God, and bringing into captivity every thought to the obedience of Christ;

2 Corinthians 10:4-5 (KJV)

What are you thinking about, and what are you not thinking about?

It is surprising how things are tremendously shifting. Afflictions that were once considered common to the older generation have become the norm among the young generation. Depression used to be common in older people, but nowadays, there is a turmoil of emotions in this generation. Depression has become a symptom of unhappiness and lack of contentment, ranging from unnecessary issues coupled with offenses. You will be shocked how some people are even offended at God for one reason or the other. Maybe you have not achieved what you wanted to achieve, but you have allowed offense and depression to abound in you. Depression, offense, anger and many other afflictions have inhabited and arrested the freedom of movement of the Word of God in your life. You have become a host of the energy and atmosphere of negativity to breed. Guard your mind; small break up, you spiral into depression; your mates are making it, you derail from God's original plan for you.

Why are we not purging unwanted stuff out of the shelves of our mind!? Some have allowed their minds to become a host and a breeding ground that produces off-springs of depression, anger, lack of contentment and all sorts of junk. You've been so accustomed to depression and offense, malice, that without anything wrong, you are depressed for being depressed. A brother offended is harder to be won than a strong city, Proverbs 18:19. Offense stands as a barrier to your deliverance. A wounded person cannot heal others; it takes total healing in you to heal others.

Most of the issues we may be depressed about can be solved by the Word pattern in contact with your spirit. Speak to yourself, encourage yourself, prophecy into your own life and if you see the results, stick to it. The involvement of the Word put in practice brings freedom to your mind. You can be free and still be chained in mind. True freedom is that which emanates from the facets of your mind. Have you ever noticed that each time you are about to be ushered into a new season, the devil will use offense, anger, pride, malice to spiritually abort the involvement of God and the jealousy of God upon your life? Everything begins to offend you big time to the extent of being offended at the progress of others. Acclimatize! When others truly hear from God, you challenge the Spirit for your incompetence. Do not allow the enemy to rob you of joy and contentment. Never allow the enemy's agitation to derail you to think God can be limited in the dealings of your affairs. God will never abandon you for any reason. Even if you sin, do not allow the devil to talk you out of the promises of God. His promises are yes and amen!

Do not rob yourself of the life you ought to live and the kingdom that must find expression in you and through you. Know yourself outside the confinements of your container [flesh]. Your thought pattern should be inspired by the Spirit and protected by the Word. Be renewed and transformed in the spirit of your mind. If you capture that you have the mind of Christ and consider it not robbery to be equal to Him: you become untouchable and unstoppable. Now let us set our minds on the things above. Most of us have made the Word of no effect by our unbelief and familiarity with God. Familiarity breeds disobedience, and it repels and vomits the involvement of God. We are filled with the Word, and the Spirit is involved in our dealings. Let not your traditions choke the Word in your life. Stop giving free access to things that you should have conquered.

Develop confidence in His plan to the extent that you do not even get upset when things do not go your way. Never create a cloud the enemy will use to inhabit himself in you. Your mind is bigger than time; it is a boundless entity! Don't allow yourself not to fully use your mind and the benefits of the Word's right thinking and application. Your mind is limitless. You can enjoy this dimension only if you break strongholds and barriers that hold you down, which keeps you stagnant and unproductive. Hide the Word of God in your heart and meditate on His Word so that you will not sin against God through your mind, rejecting the truth of your nature and identity in Christ. Fill yourself with the Word, soak and saturate yourself so that your mind begins to repel negativity on its own. Aim to attain a certain level of liberty for yourself and your mind. When your mind is attacked, transportation is disturbed. Your mind is a realm of transportation of the spiritual into the physical, which can be interrupted. The realm of conception will have been tampered with! The dimensions you carry can give your mind a robust imaginative capacity to fulfill the mandate of God.

Here's something you should carry with you today: Depression, frustration, anger, malice, offense and worry will only choke and trap the Word in you. Always engage your faith and begin to see and enjoy the benefits of your faith! You carry a dimension and nature of God to be depressed. This is a glorious season in your life you should protect jealously.

Declaration

Dear Father, I thank you for illuminating my spirit. Thank you for sending me a helper in the form of the Holy Spirit. Father, help me to pull down every stronghold and every high thing that exalts itself against your knowledge. I bring into captivity every thought to obedience to Christ. I renew my mind. I protect, and I guide my mind with all jealousy and seriousness. I engage my mind with the Word to produce evidential fruits that remain. The lenses of my mind receive healing. Every stronghold that has established and hosted itself in my mind, consciously or unconsciously, is terminated in Jesus' Name. I seal the gateway, and I take full control of the territory of my mind. I walk in total freedom in my mind. I will never be afflicted and be held hostage by my mind.

Thank you, Lord, and I release ministering spirits to bring every word I have spoken into manifestation.

Removing the lenses of other people and not comparing manuscripts

Our destinies are at the mercy of the dimension of God we know and practicalize. We need to repent from ungodly comments and unnecessary comparisons.

DAY 9

Wherefore, my beloved brethren, let every man be swift to hear, slow to speak, slow to wrath: For the wrath of man worketh not the righteousness of God

James 1:19-20 (KJV)

A fool also is full of words: a man cannot tell what shall be; and what shall be after him, who can tell him?

Ecclesiastes 10:14 (KJV)

The heart of the wise teacheth his mouth, and addeth learning to his lips.

Proverbs 16:23 (KJV)

Many times it is easy to comment; life is not fair! We compare our life with the lenses of many other people's manuscript. It may often look like it is not fair, and there is nothing you can do about it. I understand. Remember, at the back of your mind or rather in your soul, that your destiny is at the mercy of the dimension of God that you know and put into practice. You have the ability and capacity to shift your life in a whole new direction that aligns fully with the Will of God. Remember, you can do all things through Christ, who strengthens you. Start speaking right. See yourself and everything in your circumferences as how God sees it. Adhering to the constitution of heaven and kingdom principles and its jurisdiction gives you access to living a purposeful life. Therefore, giving a voice to the government of the Spirit over our life causes you to fully enjoy the benefits of the fulness of the Godhead bodily over your dealings.

Life looks unfair to those that have not laid their lives to God and the leading of the Spirit. The Holy Spirit is our advantage! The government of the Holy Spirit must govern our lives. Living an unrighteous life is a life of defeat. When God is leading you, His jealousy is well invested in you. He finds expression through you to mold you to be the exact representation that is consistent with the character of Christ in you. Never compare your life's script to someone else's and edit what is not supposed to be edited! God is not wicked or unjust to be just sitting on His throne and watching you suffer when you are His child. He wants you to prosper in all things just as your soul prospers. Be optimistic and chivalrous to learn from the school of the Spirit. Run your race. The destination is the same, but the means of teleportation and transportation are different. While this fact is clear, know that it is not in the speed that guarantees victory but waiting upon Him. They that wait upon the Lord shall renew their strength, they shall be strong and shall mount up wings as eagles. Develop confidence in His plan to the extent that you do not even get upset when things do not go your way. Do not let anything that is not of God have you.

The spiritual intelligence and experiential knowledge of knowing the life you live are not yours and that Christ lives in you gives you the advantage and assurance that nothing can look or seem unfair to God. You are above the system of this world. You attract the best of God and what the kingdom offers to those that have died in the flesh. Here in the earth realm, it is vital to living according to the demands of the Word of God. The kind of lifestyle you have can be a predominant revelation of the dimensions of God. These are evidenced by favor, mercy, and grace over your life, and you see yourself frame the substance and evidence of those things that are unseen. Only see things that are pure, honest, lovely, just, excellent and of a good report.

Here's something you should carry with you today: Your depth of comprehending the mysteries of living a good life is to be rooted in His Word and the obedience to Christ! And you will see the eradication of an unfair kind of living. Knowing your involvement with the Spirit will determine the quality of your life. A response to God's leading that is in His obedience will cause you to enjoy in abundance!

Declaration

Today I receive wisdom to know when to speak and what to speak. I receive mercy and grace. Every window of opportunity over my life is not missed in Jesus' Name. I start speaking right from today henceforth. I will never compare my script to someone else's. I run my race, and I wait upon the Lord. I know now that Christ lives in me. I involve and engage the Spirit to lead me to live a quality life full of God's presence.

This is my moment; this is my time!

Call that mountain its name; Speak to it and destroy its power

We have been given the ability to engage our faith currency into practice knowing that our faith is not the denial of circumstances, but it is not allowing circumstances to have dominion over you!

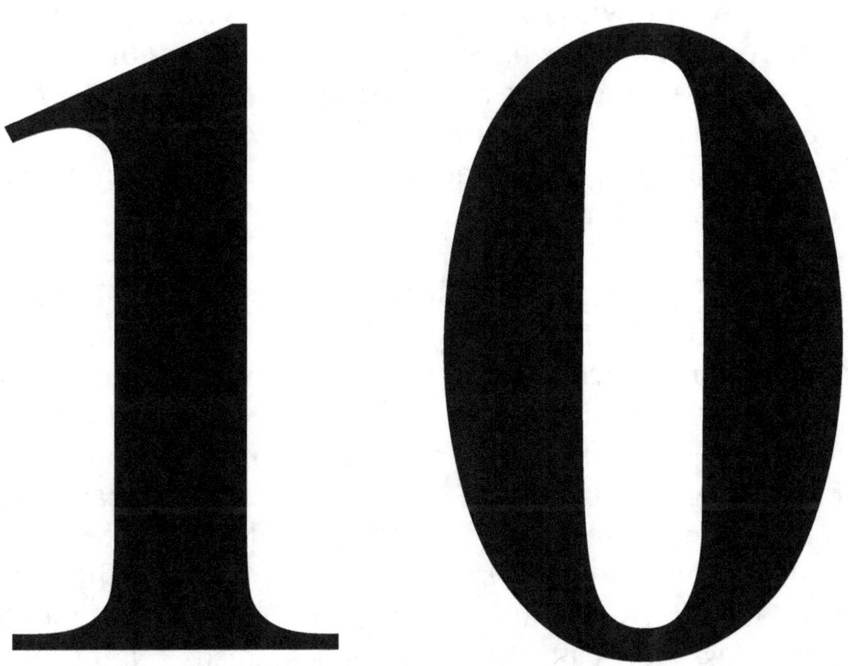

DAY 10

Who art thou, O great mountain? Before Zerubbabel thou shalt become a plain: and he shall bring forth the head-stone thereof with shoutings, crying, Grace, grace unto it.
Zechariah 4:7 (KJV)

O great mountain, move out of my way...!

You shall become insignificant. You cannot hold me down anymore. Know that no matter how big the mountain is, it shall become plain. Our God is a God of solutions. A God who makes the impossible possible. A God who makes the immovable movable. A God who makes the unbreakable breakable. A God who makes possible things humanly speaking not conceivable seen. Surely what God cannot do does not exist! We take on our priestly regalia, and we speak the dissolution of every mountain. I redeem everything you have stolen from me. You cannot attack my life again. I know who I am and who I belong to.

Any obstacle on my path shall be made plain. *Be strong O, Zerubbabel, saith the LORD for I am with you*. No matter what has been defaced before you, you shall conquer. Every mountain has a name. Call its name and destroy its power. Expose it by all means. Any obstacles before you shall disappear. Be of a good cheer; find peace in that storm because you have overcome. Every siege standing in the way of your financial freedom, ministry, spiritual walk, family, health, business, relationships and any other sphere standing to counter your progress; let it be thou removed in Jesus' Name. Stop seeing through the lens of your pain. See beyond. See the good. Capture it and move with it!

You will rebuild. Remember, it is not by might, nor by power, but by His Spirit! Restoration is coming to you. Grace is locating you; the mercies of God will speak on your behalf. Rejoice, and I say unto you rejoice! Every mountain and hill shall be made low, and the rough places plain. Anything hindering the manifestation of the call of God upon your life shall be plain. Look at the things above; He has done it for you already. Engage your faith. Even if it is as small as a mustard seed, it shall move that mountain. That mountain is a test of your faith and a confrontation of your progress. Stagger not! There is nothing new under the sun and nothing new that is unheard of. You are not alone. God is with you in that storm. Rest in the promises of God. Know that you can have challenges but do not let the same challenges have you. Develop confidence in His plan to the extent that you do not even get upset or moved when things do not go your way.

Keep looking forward, do not waver, for we walk not by sight but by faith! The sufferings of the present time are not worthy compared with the glory which shall be revealed in us. Keep holding onto your faith, your conviction and your confirmation. You are on the right track. Eventually, you shall enjoy the benefits of your faith. Do not be dismayed by the troubles. God did not guarantee you a smooth sail. There will be stones and twigs along the way, but His Word will be a lamp unto your feet and a light to your path.

Know that; blessed is he who remains steadfast under trials because when he has stood the test, he will receive a crown of life that God has promised to those who love Him. When challenges come, do not just sit and wish them to go away; you rise and seek solutions in the Word of God. Go with this; it is not unscriptural to be challenged but unscriptural to be defeated! Many are the afflictions of the righteous, but the

Lord delivers him out of them all. God wants to see the action of your reaction. Don't allow afflictions to dictate the action of your reaction to your distraction; rather, have abstraction to your breakthrough so that you can align to attract your blessings! God is turning your pain into gain. Rejoice.

Develop your faith in those mountains presented before you and see yourself triumph. This is important because engaging your faith in those circumstances or situations you are in or coming across shows that you are not in denial of circumstances. You are not allowing circumstances to have dominion over you! Know that sometimes the spiritual intelligence of suffering is one of the ways God engineers His sons. God exposes you to a level of suffering to prune you and build you up. He knows the capacity and ability that can be cultivated in you. He can never tempt you beyond what you can bear. Mountains have no dominion over you! They can be moved through faith. Use your currency that is a medium of exchange for spiritual transactions. Stay on your conviction based on who God is, the integrity of His person. He is bigger than that which you think is the end. You will never be defeated; you are dominating, you are a champion of faith, a triumphant, you are not subdued. Refuse to give up and back down because of something that tries to exalt itself. Fight a good fight of faith and put the devil to shame.

Here's something you should carry with you today: Any mountain standing against your destiny shall be exposed. Exercise your faith muscle, engage your faith and begin to enjoy the benefits of your faith. God is making every mountain plain through the ministry of His Spirit.

Declaration

Today I speak over every mountain in my life, my family, finances, academics, business, relationships, marriage, ministry, health, and in every area of my life. You cannot hold me down anymore. I command and sign off your life span warrant over my life by the power and the Spirit in me. I prevail over every affliction, over every barrier and every force of the enemy. I am victorious. Every setback in my life, I command a comeback! I call and address every mountain in my life, and I say be thou removed! Every embargo upon my life is removed and nullified in Jesus' Name.

Preparing for the exam

Examiners set exams with the assumption that we have the syllabus and we have covered it; attended school and lectures with competent teachers! And when the examination day comes; it is without mercy to those who did not put in their effort.

DAY 11

And in the morning, It will be foul weather to day: for the sky is red and lowring. O ye hypocrites, ye can discern the face of the sky; but can ye not discern the signs of the times?

Matthew 16:3 (KJV)

For many are called, but few are chosen.

Matthew 22:14 (KJV)

There's an exam set before us, which we all will soon face. There will be no exemption like we do physically in schools. Everyone is qualified, and it applies to all. The question you may want to ask yourself sincerely is; Am I preparing for the exam yet to come, or am I just deceiving myself not to prepare for anything because there is no such exam. Bear in mind that in your test is your testimony. In your persistence, there's a break through. In resistance, in your story, there's the glory from it. Let us, therefore, not be like hypocrites that can discern the face of the sky but cannot discern the signs of the times!

Those preparing will be in a better position. Be armed for battle, the climate has changed, and the atmosphere. Let us walk cautiously as wise; let us not just live our lives like civilians because our lives will become collateral damage! Wisdom is a principle thing; wisdom is a builder, and understanding of the times will establish you and set you apart. Be amongst those that qualify and pass the exam with flying colors. Be on the side of the victors. You are spiritually literate, spiritually sound, spiritually civilized, spiritually healthy, spiritually defended and above all, you are a spirit being. Know your faith will be tested by fire, and your faith will vindicate you. Let not your faith fail you.

Do not be deceived by the world system, by its grotesque parody of violence and corruption. There is no conning nor bribing. It is either you are in, or you are out. You cannot be inbetween; you cannot be lukewarm, especially in these perilous times. There are only two routes to take: the shorter one that involves corruption, leading to a fatal destination and the longer route that includes preparation, yielding and waiting on the Spirit that will teach you all things and even the deep things of God that profits your spirit. We all are eligible, and our readiness and preparedness of our hearts will determine our stand. All signs are there. It will only be denial and ignorance blinding people not to see the signs of the times we are in.

This is no time to sleep, remember for every level attained, there is a test we must pass through to be qualified. This is the preparation season. The reason for the season calls for prayerfulness. Do not be found frivolous when others are equipping themselves. The banquet is set. We all have been called, but not all will answer; only a few will respond to the call. Preparation is ongoing, do not be left out thinking there's still ample time. Talking of time, it is the unit of destiny and whatever affects your time affects your destiny. Whatever that attacks your time attacks your life and grounds you. In this case, there is no pursuing, overtaking, becoming and recovering! Take time now that is still counting to know God for yourself. Each time your time gets interrupted, you live a fruitless life.

It is dangerous not to know what to do in this season. There's an unction for preparation. Do not be found making excuses and loitering when many are focusing on the final exam. You must also partake with all your being [heart, mind, and spirit]. Your sacrifice of alignment will speak as a testament of yieldedness to the instruction of the Spirit. Be captured in the current dealings of God so as to be a contributor and a participator! Know that in this exam, it is not just enough to know God who was! There is a God who is and is to come. May we not be seen with a deficiency in accurate knowledge of the kingdom and the end times. Develop confidence in His plan to the extent that you do not even get upset when things do not go your way.

Examiners set exams assuming that you attended school and the lectures; you have the syllabus; you covered the syllabus and were taught by competent teachers. So, when the enemy attacks, he attacks and his arrows are without mercy, regardless of whether you are ready and prepared efficiently. Save yourself from the embarrassment and shame of being easily gunned down by the enemy. The syllabus to be covered was given to you way before the exam date. It is only a prudent student who prepares on time than he who thinks he can cover ground at the last minute. Unfortunately, there are principles; classes you cannot skip in the realms of the Spirit no matter how intelligent you may think you may be. The school of the Spirit is still enrolling people; admission is still on, the fee is free; it has been paid for already; just come and learn without any burden in your heart.

Here's something you should carry with you today: Prepare for the exam; the grace has been released and made available for access to the fulfillment of God's program. Align to what God is doing and make yourself an instrument and a student of the move of God.

Declaration

Father in the Name of Jesus, may I never miss the exam set before me. May I never miss heaven because of my ignorance and lack of preparedness. I know, Lord, that from my test comes my testimony. I prepare with all diligence and wisdom. Be my guide, be my will, be my way, Lord, teach me. I refuse to be blind to the times, signs and seasons we are in. I receive grace to endure and to prepare! My life is a testimony of your goodness and a pointer to many of your glory. May I develop a prayerful life to enjoy a presence-full life in the Name of Jesus!

Your approach to God

God is not a mere man that we should get familiar with; dictate and or instruct. We need to yield and key into His own will for our lives and not present to Him our own will.

DAY 12

Trust in the LORD with all thine heart; and lean not unto thine own understanding. In all thy ways acknowledge him, and he shall direct thy paths.

Proverbs 3:5 (KJV)

What is your approach to God in this season? How do you go to Him in prayer? Do you go to Him in prayer with the assumption of your plan that you believe is His plan for you? I am just bemused at how we claim maturity in the Spirit when, in fact, and reality, we are still babes!

Many may have approached God with things already, a multitude of prayers and answers they want God to sign off in their hearts. They want the same God they reverence to approve just like that. We are in the microwave generation that rejects waiting and has been crippled by the desire of being spoon-fed. Waiting on God has become waiting forever and a delay. The only way not to prolong the waiting period is to take matters into their own hands. We no longer wait like how waiters do when they serve; instead, we serve ourselves. To them, it seems like God is not interested. We go in prayer as if we are yielded to Him when we know our agenda. God looks at the sincerity of the heart.

How will you hear from Him when you have already determined a way for yourself? How will you hear when your mind and your heart is filled with your proposed answers, God should only seal without deliberation even if it will derail you from Him? Be patient; our God is a patient God.

Do not mistake patience for the delay and what will derail you as a denial. Our ways are not His ways of operation and execution. Stay a little bit longer, intercourse with Him. In that, intercourse and intimacy births visions, confirmations, convictions, dreams, revelations, clarity, and captures God's mind. You can imagine the scenario of Noah. Peradventure, Noah had not stayed in the place of prayer to hear the whole instructions and logistics; how would the ark or whatever it would have been panned out. Story for another day!

It is important to trust in the Lord our God with all our heart and not lean on our understanding, but rather to acknowledge Him to direct our paths. Let us not be wise in our own eyes; let us, therefore, come to God with absolute reliance. We often miss out on God when we do not rely on His sovereignty and lean on our limited human understanding. Our approach to Him determines our sincerity! Do not hustle with God because there is no hassle with Him. They that wait upon the Lord shall renew their strength. Be patient until clarity is cultivated from the place of intimacy and intercourse. Never go to Him with what you think you will hear. Do not go ahead of Him; let Him lead and use you through. Draw near to Him, and He will draw near to you.

Here's something you should carry with you today; Be sincere in your approach to God and your quest for the kingdom. Lean on Him, linger in His presence and become entwined to Him.

Declaration

Lord, I come to your throne of grace that I may receive mercy. I put my trust in you. Help me be sincere to demonstrate yieldedness to the fruit of my lips. I trust in your judgement and not my will. I lean not on my understanding. I acknowledge you, Father. Direct my path, Lord. May my relationship with you be about seeking your Will, your kingdom and not advocating for my will to prevail. Teach me to be patient. I have an absolute reliance on you. From today, I wait on you in my secret place. And I know I win by waiting on your Lordship, Lord. I draw closer to you from today.

Seek God for yourself

It is our time to take our spiritual responsibility to grow in the Spirit and to develop an intimate relationship with our Father.

DAY 13

But seek ye first the kingdom of God, and his righteous-
ness; and all these things shall be added unto you.
                                        Matthew 6: 33 (KJV)

For do I now persuade men, or God? Or do I seek to please
men? For if I yet pleased men, I should not be the servant
of Christ.
                                        Galatians 1:10 (KJV)

HE that dwelleth in the secret place of the most High shall
abide under the shadow of the Almighty.
                                        Psalms 91:1 (KJV)

In these difficult times we are in, many are now running to different men of God asking— "Man of God, pray for me. Man of God, prophesy into my life. Man of God, seek God on our behalf and tell us what God wants us to do." Well, this is the man of God syndrome that has plagued the church and this generation. I am not saying there is anything wrong with this. Still, there's everything wrong with this when it becomes the only thing and source you wait for. If you depend on them without your effort to seek and hear for yourself as your prophet and priest, then there's a very big problem. We have become so accustomed to not wanting to seek God for ourselves. It feels exhausting. We have become a microwave generation, a generation that always wants to be spoon-fed with everything and anything. The days to play church are over. We are in dangerous times that call for sensitivity. Those with a relationship will stand and draw strength from having intercourse and intimacy with Him in the secret place.

It is that time we begin to take our spiritual responsibility. God is calling everyone to the place of encounters for personal experiences with Him. One on one mentorship and intense tutorship that activates His manifest presence. God has always made Himself available to you so you can seek Him for yourself, although He will not force Himself on you against your own will. The choice, therefore, is yours and yours alone to take! Let us not be spiritual bullies to men of God. Yes, they have been sent for us but let us not misuse their ministry of help and take it for granted. Since God knew we need the five-fold ministry, this, however, does not eliminate and nullify the fact and truth that He has called us all to the secret place to fellowship with Him. Not only men of God can hear God or seek God; we all can mature to that dimension by reason of fellowship. Try it and see, taste and see that He is God. He works in you both to will and to do of His good pleasure.

We all have a part to play and a part of accounting for. Did you know that you can neglect your biggest platform and function outside the jurisdiction of your relevance? Did you know? The biggest platform or stage is your secret place. If you ever desire to be great, relevant, influential and valuable, attend to your secret place. Tend to your secret place. We have become so ignorant that we need to be fed as much as we feed our physical body as spiritual beings. Balance your body's three-course meals that you always adhere to the course meals for your spirit. Start feeding your spirit, create time and an environment. In this atmosphere, an intimate relationship with God beyond being corporate is established. He that dwelleth in the secret place of the Most High shall abide under the shadow of the Almighty.

Do not be gravitationally pulled by the circumstances of this cosmos. Why have you entertained that which you should have outgrown as a babe? Let your mindset shift from total dependency and allow His will to be your obsession. We need to enter into our spiritual maturity and encounter God at a personal level. Let us stop these charismatic gymnastics from making ourselves feel good when we are not transforming in reality. Facetime with God, not just with humanity only! Stop fellowshipping with smoke [worldly trends] and start fellow-shipping with fire. When you start maturing in the things of the Spirit, then God can entrust you with a greater sense of power and access to deeper realms in the Spirit. Create a track record in the Spirit. There's a greater intensity of His presence that is available for us to encounter this season. Learn to raise your altar of prayer and intimacy. Mysteries of the kingdom will be revealed based on your consistency. Honor the people God uses, but do not misuse them.

Here's something you should carry with you today: Learn to take spiritual responsibility, exercise your spiritual muscles and senses, and see yourself grow. The days for dependency are over; God is calling your [you] altar, He is knocking at your door. Do you hear Him knocking and calling? He is at the door!

Declaration

From today, I exercise my authority as a son to seek first my Father and not just depend on the ministry of help. I take my spiritual responsibility from today, and I begin to play my part. I begin to seek you, Father, knowing this is a vital ingredient to a relevant living. I now know that seeking you is proof of my dependency and a testimony of true worship. Help me, Father, as I mature in the things of the Spirit and as I begin to sincerely seek you with all thy might and in the spirit. From today I honor the ministry of help, and I do not misuse them for my benefit. I begin to dwell in your presence from today henceforth. I revive my secret place. And today, I begin to fellowship with the Spirit, with all intimacy, brokenness and with a contrite heart. As I raise my alter of prayer today, may I begin to burn for you.

Offer value through gaining spiritual wisdom, understanding and knowledge

Building yourself in your secret place allows for weight and stamina to be developed in all your life stages.

DAY 14

Through wisdom is an house builded; and by understanding it is established: And by knowledge shall the chambers be filled with all precious and pleasant riches.

Proverbs 24:3-4 (KJV)

Be careful not to fall and not to misguide yourself foolishly. Be wise, walk circumspectly. It may seem daunting when many are focused on making statements and deriving their confidence [pride of life] by parading with all kinds of material possessions. They have no strategy for maintenance and regenerating. Be calm. Know that it is far much better to be wasted by and of God and gain treasures in the kingdom than to be wasted in this world trying to acquire riches. Your reward will surely come. Those who are of the kingdom know that He always supplies our need according to His riches in glory by Christ Jesus!

As for you, you offer value! Value in the dealings with God and influence in the things of the Spirit. Your value is your virtue, and virtue is the closeness and same character and nature of Christ. Offer your value and allow that influence to cause everything you touch to prosper. Remember, your head is anointed. The contact of the oil flowing through your head with things in the physical realm will cause instant attraction! The truth is that it is better to stand with God and be condemned by the world than to stand with the world and be condemned by God. Possessions and wealth obtained without wisdom, without sense and without the Spirit's backing to sustain only leads to poverty. What is it that is backing you?

What is the spirit behind your success? We only grow when we understand the ways of the kingdom and the Will of our Father. Allow your consciousness to be invested in the kingdom. Many are living a life of breakthrough [onetime event] instead of a life of favor [continuous overflow]. To achieve a life of favor, you need to allow the oil upon your head to find expression. Allow the kingdom pattern to be your lifestyle, and see goodness overload and overflow bountifully from all dimensions.

Never build without surveying and securing the place of building and the building itself. For the Word makes us understand, *"For which of you, intending to build a tower; sitteth not down first, and counteth the cost, whether he have sufficient to finish it? Lest haply, after he hath laid the foundation, and is not able to finish it, all that behold it begin to mock him," Luke 14:28-29 (KJV).* Take your time. It is ok to permit yourself to take time to grow. Your situation is transitory. Imagine after building, and you realize the foundation is faulty! Wealth gotten by vanity shall be diminished, but he that gathereth by labor shall increase. Build value and give value to those things you are seeking for than to seek value in material things. Our value is not in human-made things; our value is in God. If we are hidden with Christ in God, then we are valuable. Rest in the assurance that all these things will be added unto you when you seek first His kingdom. Approval from God precedes the approval of man! Wisdom is a principal thing, wisdom builds, and understanding establishes. Remember He giveth power to make wealth, so build value first, and all these things will be drawn to you since they were made for you, not you made for them. First, believe that He is a rewarder of them that diligently seek Him. Stay faithful to Him: *"That the trial of your faith, being much more precious than of gold that perisheth, though it be tried with fire, might be found unto praise and honour and glory at the appearing of Jesus Christ:" 1 Peter 1:7.*

Pursue the ultimate and get the immediate!

Be value-oriented. The presence of the Name of Jesus gives value to your dealings. Many may mock you now, but God, our Father, will make you! Rest knowing that it is the end that will speak for you and be fruitful.

Here's something you should carry with you today: Be encouraged, be not ashamed of the stage you are in your life. If you honor the process, God will honor His promises that are yea and Amen, unto the glory of God by us. This is a testament to endurance.

Declaration

Today I choose to walk circumspectly as wise. I offer value; I offer influence because I come from above. I prefer to be wasted by God and of God than to be wasted of this world. My consciousness is heavily invested in the kingdom, and the rest will attach themselves to the oil upon my head. I believe that my Father, who is in Heaven, will supply all my needs not according to my needs but according to His riches in glory! I trust the legitimate processes God is putting me through and tutoring me. I know all things worketh together for my good because I love Him, and I have been called according to His purpose. Lord, you are the portion of my inheritance and my cup. On the solid Word of God, I build today the Word that is quick and powerful, sharper than any edged sword. The Spirit of God leads me. I receive knowledge, the Spirit of wisdom and understanding in Jesus' Name.

Amen.

Being led and
looking onto the Master builder

Having the right understanding with God is important despite what man may require of you, and every other thing will melt and become irrelevant before you.

DAY 15

When a man's ways please the LORD, he maketh even his enemies to be at peace with him.

Proverbs 16:7 (KJV)

And we know that all things work together for good to them that love God, to them who are called according to his purpose.

Romans 8:28 (KJV)

Do not be derailed by those that despise you. Heaven did not design for you to be liked by everybody. Even Jesus, the son of God, was despised by many who handled the luxury of religion. But if God be for you, who can be against you. In this life you can never find all people liking you, never, it is simply not possible! But that should not dictate how you must live your life. Allow influence to draw them to what you carry. Let the oil upon your head speak for you and attract them to you. Many may not like you or support you. Still, a certain fact is that when you carry value and influence, they are left with no choice but to target and be drawn to you and benefit from what you have, the oil upon your head, the anointing you carry and the grace that speaks on your behalf and the God of your life. When a man's ways please the Lord, He makes even His enemies be at peace with him. Your enemies are needed for your progress. They are necessary for you to exercise praying for them and the power you carry to bless them to be exercised. They need you to be blessed; understand that.

Do not also despise those that despise you. You are only breaking scriptures. Do not interfere with the blessings that should come their way. Believe me, why will people like you when the jealousy of God has been heavily invested upon you. It always looks like God is unfair because it is like He only loves you more than anybody. So, when your enemies hate you; please, have a heart for them and understand them. You are born of God, and you know God. And they cannot seem to shake off that truth! Bare and understand their focal point. Who will not be offended; it is not easy if you were in their shoes, seeing you blessed! Love them and do good to them, and your reward will be great. The greatest expression and manifestation of love are rewarded when you love those who hate you and those with no room and capacity to love you back and bless those that curse you.

Remember, all things work together for good to them that love Him and to them that are called according to His purpose. You are the prestige and pride of God. You may want to ask your-self how God will prepare a table before you in the presence of your enemies. The table has to be prepared for them to be witnesses. Their approval will not change what God has said about you. It is your purpose that should navigate you and not likes! Genuine hunger for more of God will cause you not to pay attention to things that do not matter. Keep focusing on your Father's agenda and purpose and practice the kingdom's nature to them that despise you. Love should be expressed when hate is dominant to cancel that spirit and for that spirit to insecure its power.

Here's something you should carry with you today: Repent and refrain from seeking the approval of man. Keep steering the waters inside you.

Declaration

Lord help me so that my ways may please you. May I not focus on those that despise me, but rather, may I walk in love to always bless those that hate me because they depend on my blessings and prayers. Father, I thank you for heavily investing your jealousy upon me. Help me to develop a heart for my enemies. May I not hate them. May I walk in love. I believe that I am the prestige and pride of my Father. From today I am not moved by the number of likes; I am moved by the compassion that my Father deposited in me, which is of Him.

Breaking the spirit that sponsors failure

We are born of God, and we carry the Spirit of God in us and failure is not in the nature and character of our Father.

16

DAY 16

For as he thinketh in his heart, so is he: Eat and drink, saith he to thee; but his heart is not with thee.
Proverbs 23:7 (KJV)

Examine yourselves, whether ye be in the faith; prove your own selves. Know ye not your own selves, how that Jesus Christ is in you, except ye be reprobates?
2 Corinthians 13:5 (KJV)

(For the weapons of our welfare are not carnal, but mighty through God to the pulling down of strong holds;) Casting down imaginations, and every high thing that exalteth itself against the knowledge of God, and bringing into captivity every thought to the obedience of Christ;
2 Corinthians 10:4-5 (KJV)

You are not a failure, and you have never been one. You are too loaded to fail! This applies to those who believe and to those who can receive to allow the character and nature of God to find expression in them. Stop poisoning your mind. You've got the mind of Christ in you. You cannot afford to be a failure because of your spiritual ignorance and your spiritual illiteracy. No, you cannot. Heaven has not invested so much and deposited so much in you only to fail. No! However, and surprisingly, many have operated in ignorance and failed not because it is their nature but because they went outside their nature and rejected to invest in knowledge. You have the legislation to exempt yourself from being a candidate.

Failure in its simplest is operating outside the jurisdiction of your relevance, living a life without Him [irrelevance]. If you do not accept and confess what God says you are and acknowledge it: you cannot mirror and obtain. Remember, you were created in His likeness and image. The same Spirit present at the beginning, hovering upon the face of the waters that made all that we see now, is the same in you. By telling yourself, you're a failure; you are simply breaking scripture and saying God is a failure Himself. By affirming His Word believing and receiving, you provoke a character, an identity, a nature in you; you carry of God. You provoke realms, a fountain of dimensions of the possibilities and provisions of God. A Spirit-filled life is key to victory and breaking the limitations of that mind that sees failure. Begin to unlock the success that needs to birth forth from you. Resist that mindset that wants to bind you and draw you back. Remember, what you don't resist will persist! If you sow a thought, you reap an action; sow an action, reap a habit, sow a habit, reap a character, and sow a character, reap a destiny. Sow the Word of God in your mind, and your destiny will flourish.

Never allow your prayer warrior [mind] to be defeated and discouraged. You are a record-breaker, a pacesetter, a game-changer. Do you believe it? Can you fathom it? Have you captured the picture and the purpose God has for you to venture and feature into your future? Then go beyond the limitation of your thoughts, the limitation of your environment, your family, your generation and anything and everything that you think you cannot do and or achieve. Let it cross your mind, sink into your mind and spirit for access to be given to break every stronghold that wants to hold you down and exalt itself against the knowledge of God. Allow the flow for possibilities to become a reality. As a man thinketh in his heart, so he is. Do not allow your thoughts to limit your results. As far as your eyes see, so shall you have.

You are born of a God who can do exceedingly abundantly above all that you ask or think, according to the power that worketh in you. Start seeing yourself differently; you are peculiar, the righteousness of God in Him. Know the difference between failure as a person and failure as an event. Never build monuments on failure. Do not allow the progress of other people to make you think you are failing. God makes everything beautiful in its time.

Here's something you should carry with you today: What happens to you, your mind, perception, and point of view determine what will happen for you. Explore the endless realms of possibilities you already have access to.

Declaration

I decree and declare that from today I exercise and walk in my true nature. I am loaded, I have been preloaded, and I am always reloaded. I am not a failure, and I have never been. I am spiritually civilized of my nature. Failure is not my portion because I have the Word in me. The Spirit of God is working in me on the inside to will and doing of His good pleasure. I have the mind of Christ in me. I cannot be defeated and dejected. I pull down every stronghold that wants to exalt itself against the knowledge of God in the Name of Jesus. I am relevant in my generation. My life is a testimony of your overloaded goodness. I begin to see myself differently and just the same way God sees me. I am not limited because the greater one lives inside me; the unlimited and invincible God is inside me. I am the image and the likeness of God; therefore, I am victorious! I excel in all things and all ramifications yea, I have a goodly heritage. I receive healing to my perception, and I experience a change in position in Jesus' Mighty Name!

Infilling and the servicing of the Spirit

Aligning ourselves in order for the Spirit to service us, direct us, guide us and fill us through the journey is important for our fire not to go down. The Spirit always rekindles!

DAY 17

For this cause we also, since the day we heard it, do not cease to pray for you, and to desire that ye might be filled with the knowledge of his will in all wisdom and spiritual understanding. That ye might walk worthy of the Lord unto all pleasing, being fruitful in every good work, and increasing in the knowledge of God;

Colossians 1:9-10 (KJV)

And I have filled him with the spirit of God, in wisdom, and in understanding, and in knowledge, and in all manner of workmanship,

Exodus 31:3 (KJV)

Not only gadgets have engines, but sons of God also have engines too and require maintenance. Renew the oil of your engine. Fill it. Top it up. Fuel the tank of your spirit and make sure your radiator is functioning properly and is filled with water. The journey you are embarking on needs your engine and parts to be good. You cannot afford to be going about your dealings or the journey and errands with a reserve tank. Sooner or later, it will be empty, and you will get stuck along the way. You cannot dry up. No, not in this season and in these perilous times! Fellowship…

The scriptures mentioned and emphasized several times the need and essence of being filled. Being filled enables you to introduce and be a candidate of the presence, the manifest presence of God through the Holy Spirit. There's a need for you to be filled, especially in this season. Make yourself available because God wants you to be filled with power, with the

Spirit of the Lord, justice and courage. Be filled. The journey to be embarked on needs those filled with knowing what to do and not to be captured and drowned in this world's system. If you are not filled, anything and everything will fill itself in you without being aware. Do not be too conscious of filling alcohol in place of the Holy Spirit. It is better to be drunk in the Spirit than to be drunk in beverages. Being drunk in alcoholic beverages does not take you far and does not last, but being drunk in the Spirit takes you further and drives you far. Wake up, sons of God. Your Father wants to fill you with His Spirit in wisdom, in understanding, in knowledge and all manner of workmanship. You can accelerate at the speed and fuel of God through being connected to the source [God].

Stay connected to the source [Spirit] and keep drawing from Him to see greatness be unlocked in you, vast possibilities and potentials to find access for expression. Make yourself available. Many of us are called but may not walk in the ministry we have been called into until we develop the environment and atmosphere of being filled, a prayer life where God can commune with us expressly. The place of being filled allows us to journey beyond humanity and operate above this world's elements. We journey from the earth to the divine nature and ability that enables us to carry out God's assignment. When you are filled with the Spirit, your weaknesses, your youthful strengths, are exchanged with the strength of God. You will no longer be relying on and going about your dealings with a reserve tank. He fills you up when you connect to His source that never runs dry. Pray!

Avoid making spiritual abortions! Guard your progress, guard your ground, protect your secret place. Be wise. Mercy and grace brought you where you are. Guard yourself against distractions. Do not allow yourself to get to a point you rely on and function with a reserve tank. How then will you give to others when you are not overflowing? How will you give from what is not enough and where you are trying to survive and live off? Be filled! It is the only way to avoid shortages and from your engine to heat up and breakdown. Be fired up! Use this time to refill so that you don't give from your reserve tank but from the running over of your cup. Preserve your reserve!

Here's something you should carry with you today: Renew your engine oil, fuel your tank, make sure your radiator is filled with water so as not to heat and breakdown—service all the parts that need service for you not to faint ahead.

Declaration

From today I will continually go back to the place of being filled with the Spirit of God in wisdom, understanding, knowledge and all manner of workmanship. I draw closer to Him as He draws closer to me. I fellowship with the Spirit always. When I pray, the Spirit will fill me up. I am anointed, and my cup runneth over. I guard my secret place, and I stay connected to the Spirit at all times. Develop in me the hunger to fellowship and stay filled with accelerating in the Spirit. I connect to your source Lord. Fill me up, fill me up till I overflow; I want to run over!

Encouraging
yourself in the Lord

Things might not look like the visions you wrote down when you received them in the secret place, but do not fast forward the process of building if you desire to see the fruition and conceptualization of the visions.

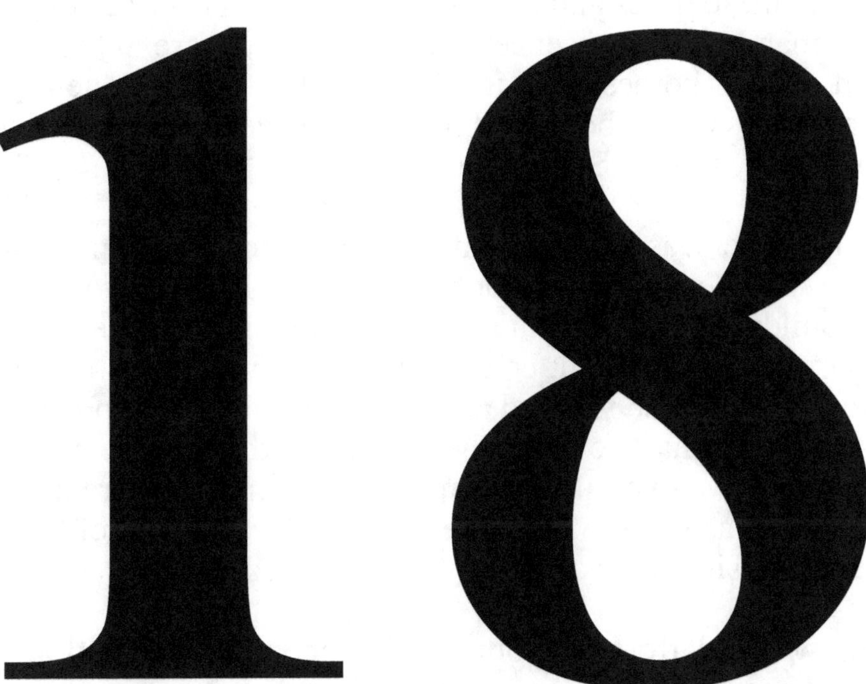

DAY 18

Therefore, my beloved brethren, be ye steadfast, unmovable, always abounding in the work of the Lord, forasmuch as ye know that your labour is not in vain in the Lord.
                                    1 Corinthians 15:58 (KJV)

Be wise in this season. Be careful; do not be deceived by social media. We are in dangerous times. Anyone can preach, anyone can prepare a good message; anyone can be a great teacher. Many can clap you to your grave and your downfall. Do not be too focused on delivering rhema without true transformation. Your progress is not measured by the number of people who respond to your posts. Have you ever noticed that in these times and seasons we are in, it is very difficult to command media presence? Inasmuch people are in the comfort of their homes; still, it is difficult for them to tune in and watch messages about God. Rather it is very easy to connect to worldly trends. Strange but true…

This is the season we are in that only those that know their God shall be strong. Do not be derailed to let go of your focus on building. Do not be in a hurry to announce yourself before your time and without content in your container. In this generation, we are so focused and driven by wanting to prove that we have rhema; we carry the revelation that no one has ever captured. We overtake our fathers in Faith and discredit their messages as shallow. Beware of premature exposure! Do not be responsible for your doors being closed.

Allow the platform of your secret place to be the platform to announce you by the aura of the manifest presence of God that emanates from your being. Build your secret place first. The biggest platform, our altar, is calling us. Influence, value and virtue are born from the secret place, the place of intimacy, communion and fellowship. Build your relationship with God so that you develop a track record in the Spirit where God begins to entrust you with mysteries. Be so radical with your faith. Remember Noah? He looked like a crazy fellow until it started to rain; keep building. Do you want to be great? Keep preparing for it is not suddenly stumbled upon; it is prepared for. There is no success story without being diligent in what you do. Be patient. Social media is not your Holy Spirit! Social media can be the greatest killer of destinies, visions, purpose when the focus is misappropriated. Never allow yourself to be distracted by likes and followers. Focus on the authenticity of the spread of the kingdom.

When nobody views, likes, shares, retweets, advertise or comments, do not be discouraged. Keep your diligence and consistency in check and balanced, and you will break resistance. For this cause, we faint not. Be steadfast, unmovable, and always abounding in the work of the Lord. Your labor is not in vain. Remember having many likes is not a guarantee and a measurement that you will build a great church, organization, empire, business and any other great thing you can think of. Keep doing your part; your consistency will break resistance and will bring you to the right audience. Keep inspiring them until you become valuable. Allow your credibility, availability and reliability to deliver, announce you. We are all anointed for a different and unique audience. Cook yourself in the secret place. Be prayerful and keep pushing until that ministry in you comes alive.

Here's something you should carry with you today: Honor the building process, and God will honor His promise. Don't be too quick to give up when no one shows interest. This is a testament to a dimension of conviction and confirmation.

Declaration

I receive wisdom in this season to be steadfast, unmovable and always abounding in the work of the Lord, for I know that my labor is not in vain. I refuse to announce myself before my time prematurely. I yield to the Holy Spirit for direction, reproach and teaching. Lord, I believe my secret place will announce me and create great platforms for me. I build my altar. Social media will not dictate my rising. Social media is not the Holy Spirit. God will announce my arrival. I live above this world and its corrupting influences. I stay focused on my conviction until my ministry comes alive. I am anointed and appointed for such a time.

Cultivating
the dialect of love

Love is the expression of your spirit, the evidence of the depth of God that has found expression and is constantly at work in you!

DAY 19

Beloved, let us love one another: for love is of God; and every one that loveth is born of God, and knoweth God

1 John 4:7 (KJV)

The garment of love…

The ministry of love… The dialect of love…

Some say love is a set of emotions and behaviors characterized by intimacy, affection, attraction, passion, commitment, trust, protectiveness and many others. Yes, it is. But love is a language. A language that should be taught, expressed and communicated. Love needs to be properly dispensed and apportioned. Have you ever loved someone or people, and in turn, you were mistreated with unpleasant attitudes? Are you tired of loving people and getting hurt? Well, the bible says we should love one another. If you want to join God and walk with Him, start loving! Before you do anything, start loving. Everyone deserves your love. Love is a language that, when misinterpreted and misunderstood with evidence of characters of emotions and behaviors, amounts to nothing and, in some cases, can be fatal.

Love is simply an expression of your spirit, which is inevitable not to give when you're spiritual! Above all virtues, put on love. The garment of love. We love because He first loved us. Love is a language that must be understood and comprehended. Many have misused love as an arrogant presumption of privilege. Did you know many people, including you and me, can heal or be healed by the expression of love than by the gift of healing itself? You are also a physician. You have to be determined. Be found doing what your Father is doing, that is, to love under any circumstance. Love is rewarded when you love those who hate you and those who cannot love you back. When you love expecting nothing in return, you are guaranteed a great reward. You are a product of God, an offspring of God raised by love. Do not allow yourself to be brought up by something that did not raise you! Love is an act of obedience. Be rooted and established in love.

The world needs love. You cannot claim to love God and not exhibit love. It is simply not possible, maybe if you are deceiving yourself! For God is love. Lack of love is merely an affliction, an affliction that does not want you to prosper and be above the system of this world. Are you afflicted? Love is surely the answer. Yes, love. Many pray, and yet they do not love. You will be surprised how most of the issues we are facing can be solved by more love, the exhibition of love. Remember, if you do not love, you detach yourself from God. Whoever loves others has fulfilled the constitution of heaven and the kingdom legislation. If the world knows love, then many people will know God. You cannot say you love God yet hate your brother or your sister. You are simply a liar and cannot love God, this is what the scriptures say, and you will be breaking scripture. Be sincere with love; it covers a multitude of sins.

You become more like God when you love, and when love is received. Love that is received heals and creates an atmosphere of recovery. Have you ever visited a loved one, and you constantly stay with them throughout? In most cases, they quickly recover because of the love being expressed and them receiving your love. Whosoever lives in love lives in God. Many claim to have received God, but the proof of receiving God is love. Love is the highest form of blessings! Do you believe that? It is God we will be proving we do not fathom when we do not love. This world can be a better place if we exhibit and express love more.

No more excuses not to love because it was misappropriated. This is more reason why you should love because we do not need reasons to love. Imagine if every one of us needed to give reasons why God should love them with the state of their hearts now. How many would pass the interview? Make yourself a portal that stands as material for the blessings of God. Offenses may and will come; anger may take over, frustration may lead, hate may inhabit, enemies may emerge, but love remains your armor. Remember, the glory of a king is in overlooking a matter! We are kings; we walk in love.

Please permit me to tell you a short experiment I did. I kept many potatoes in a bowl on my kitchen counter. We were in the winter season where no moisture, sun, water, or anything can happen, especially inside the house. It was extremely cold. Long story short, all the potatoes started germinating so much and so fast that I could not cook them anymore. They kept growing and growing to the extent that I began looking for a garden to plant them so that they would not go to waste. The lesson was to see whether things around me, my environment responded to love. Well, it worked. Love is the key and very important. The environment can respond to love; animals respond to love; nature responds to love; humanity responds to love. Therefore, do not withhold the God dimension of love in you.

Here's something you should carry with you today: Learn the love language and heal your surroundings. Love is our habitation, an atmosphere, recreation and replication of heaven on earth!

Declaration

Henceforth, I wear the garment of love, and I speak the language of love in all my actions. I will begin to communicate and express love properly and in a way that will be received. I represent that which is in my Spirit and me. I put on the virtue of love. I am an exhibitor of love. I will start loving people from today because God first loved me. I overlook those that mistreat me because I know a king's glory is to ignore a matter. I will love my neighbor as I love myself. Everything around me responds to love. I am a channel of blessings because I dispense and apportion love. I am a well that springs forth love! I will change the world with my love and make it a better place. For God so loved the world, and He gave, I will give and express the love of God springing forth from my wells.

Rebuilding
faulty foundations

God is not an affair we run to only when we are in dire need! He is the horn, and the seal of our salvation; the lifter of our head, and He must always be our stronghold in all things when we seek Him.

DAY 20

Seek the LORD and his strength, seek his face continually.
1 Chronicles 16:11 (KJV)

Seek ye the LORD while he may be found, call ye upon him while he is near:
Isaiah 55:6 (KJV)

That they should seek the Lord, if haply they might feel after him, and find him, though he be not far from every one of us:
Acts 17:27 (KJV)

One certain fact and testimony of our walk with God needs to be revisited. We need to go back to the foundation—the precision of His character, His Person, His nature and His logos.

Speaking with all honesty and repentance, each one of us has been a prayer warrior at some point. We have deceived ourselves so much to think we are so spiritual and we are growing spiritually. Yet, we are prompted to pray by our circumstances that have choked us and made us question the sovereignty of God. We then resort to prayer as the only option only because we see no way of escape. Instead of seeking the things above, we seek the things of the earth. For us to pray, God has to guarantee that we will benefit and that He will fulfill His side of the bargain. Believers, Christians who has bewitched us? Seeking God is for our good; it is for us to transform into our true identity. We are students of the Spirit; let us not mock the sovereignty of God and take His love towards us for granted.

We have not yet come to the fulness and the spiritual civilization of who God is and our contribution and participatory role as a body of Christ! I come in love, but my heart bleeds. Most of us claim to know God at a personal level, yet our secret places are neglected. My heart bleeds! We have the propensity to be very spiritual when in need. We are known for praying for many hours, but we are not known for hearing the voice of God.

Why are we too materialistic with God? We have refused to be wasted by God. Being wasted by God and being wasted of Him pays. We no longer have intimacy with the Holy Spirit to command results. Our secret places are being made barren because of no sacrifice of fellowship to carry a seed that brings about the pregnancy of His intimacy. The primary assignment of us praying is for us to be changed, and our needs will change. How then do we stay in power when we are not always in contact with what gives us access to power itself! Let us live lives of answers and avoid an arena of questions about our Christianity and our powerlessness. The distance between your position now and your destination is dependent on your revelation. Everything you will ever need is in Matthew 6:33. Check yourself, evaluate yourself. How is your foundation like? Many pray heaven into existence and manifestation because of where they are operating from and prompting them. It is not about what you are saying; it is where you are saying it from that matters. Because of God's mercies and His grace, He always supplies our needs not according to our needs but according to His riches in glory. He is a merciful God. But we need to grow up. The devious times we are in calls for those with a relationship to stand strong.

Seek him while He can be found. Do not be deceived by prayer warriors until you have seen their fruits and the tangibility of their seeds of faith, the substance and evidence of the aura and pattern of the presence they host. Then you will know who is who. Power can be faked, but presence cannot be faked! A man of presence manifests encounters and experiences and has journeyed beyond just prayers but to the extent of discovering the divinity hidden inside him and coming in contact with God. We have to come to a point where God [you] begin to fellowship with God beyond the capacity flesh can comprehend. This is now the intercourse and intimacy with God, and He is calling us to this dimension. We have developed an extra-curricular kind of affair with God. It is only when we desire a breakthrough that we intercourse with Him in prayer. When there's fire on the mountain, maybe overdue husband, wife, job, business, visa and finances, among many others, we call on God for rescue. Many are hiding under this blanket of needs and prayer points. We come to the throne of grace to obtain what we need, and we leave. No longer do we stay to fellowship with grace and mercy to build us up.

We are prayer warriors, but for a moment, we are consistent, but for a moment, we are diligent. Still, for a moment, we are dedicated, but for a moment, we are disciplined. Still, for a moment, we are deliberate but for a moment, and we sacrifice but for a moment. What manner of Christianity are we practicing of being part-time believers, trying to con God? Corruption everywhere, even in high places. We are fortunate that our Father is the embodiment of love Himself.

Here's something you should carry with you today: Repent if need be from our shameful ways. God cannot be mocked. This is a heart cry for true transformation and a testament calling for true repentance.

Declaration

Lord, I repent from my old ways. I put on a new self. I want to genuinely seek you not because of what I need from you, but because of who you are, Lord, because of your Lordship over my life. I want to develop a sincere relationship with you, not an affair. For I know if I seek you and your righteousness all these things I long so much for, and need will be added unto me. May I not be centered on my needs but on seeking your face. May I be among those that genuinely fellowship and worship you in Spirit and truth. I want to go all-in with you with all my heart, mind and soul. I do not want to waver. Let my fellowship with you not be centered on needs but my true worship.

The testament of obedience

Obedience always paves way for abundance and creates an advantage to be connected in the Spirit! It is a sin-free zone where distinctions in life are birth forth.

DAY 21

For rebellion is as the sin of witchcraft, and stubbornness is as iniquity and idolatry. Because thou hast rejected the word of the LORD, he hath also rejected thee from being king.

1 Samuel 15:23 (KJV)

The equation of obedience…The testament of obedience…Culminating obedience to Christ!

The sin of man is one! It is disobedience… Do you agree? Every other sin is an offspring and a series of disobedience. We need to understand that as long there's a man to obey the instructions of God, there's always a God to eliminate destructions. One man's disobedience made many sinners, and by the obedience of one, many were made righteous. Obedience may not be very appealing, but it is the mystery behind distinctions in life. You cannot enjoy lasting progress without proven to be obedient. You need an elastic mentality and character to remain disciplined and obedient to eat the good of the land. If you are convinced in your heart that you are walking in obedience to Christ, then glory to God! Prompt obedience in the Lord is a requirement and a proof of faith and confidence in God.

But if you walk in obedience, you will not do certain things that you do. Do your background check; we are walking in disobedience in some way or the other. Come back to obedience to Christ. Get obedience right and settle the matter of sin once and for all. Prune every branch that sponsors disobedience. Every sin is an offspring of your disobedience to God.

This exposes you to the devil to temper with your obedience because the hedge would have been broken. Obedience can set you free. Decide today to start walking in obedience. We do not attain obedience; we constantly walk in obedience! It is a personal walk and not a corporate activity. Disobedience breeds all manner of sin. Remember, there's a way which seemeth right unto a man, but the end thereof are the ways of death [destruction]. Sin will checkmate you from obedience, and you will end up involved in many things because of disobedience.

We have spiritually aborted many destinies and destinations. Many of us; our habitation is disobedience. We swim in it, glory in it, and we are comfortable living in it. And when we pray, we want God not to deal with it. Well, prayer is not a substitute for disobedience. We have become employees, hostages and agents of disobedience. We have to draw a line of enough is enough and go back on track. We have gone far and off the grid from hearing the call of God. Obedience is key to walking in abundance. If you obey His voice and keep His covenant, then you shall be a peculiar treasure unto Him above all people. It is always better and rewarding to wait while in obedience than to rush while in disobedience. Unfortunately, there is no fear and reverence; we walk in series and dimensions of sin. We cover our sins with prayer.

We have become cultivators of sin. Rebellion is a sin of witchcraft, and stubbornness is iniquity and idolatry. And because we have rejected the word of the Lord, we have rejected Him being king. Repent. The kingdom of God is at hand. God is calling you to obedience. Do not ignore His call. It is never too late to turn back lest Satan should get an advantage of us, for we are not ignorant of his devices. For some, the propensity for familiarity is bad. Change for the better.

Obedience attracts favor in the Spirit. Your obedience is an advantage for you to be connected in the Spirit, for we are the circumcision who worship God in the Spirit and rejoices in Christ Jesus. We have no confidence in the flesh because we are dead in the flesh and alive in the Spirit. Although we are in this world, we are not of this world; this world's system cannot allure us to be disobedient by any means. Be vigilant. For it is at our owner's risk; costly and fatal in some cases to be contrary to the voice of the Spirit. Obedience is a weapon you use against the enemy's devious ways when he tries to derail you. When you obey God, you trust that He leads you to endless opportunities that, in turn, make your destiny. Obedience is for your convenience.

Here's something you should carry with you today: Obedience is better than sacrifice, knowing that giving an ear to the enemy allows for disobedience to be inevitable.

Declaration

Father, from today I walk in obedience. Anything and everything that led me to disobey your leading is nullified in Jesus' Name. I have been made righteous, and so I walk, and I live a righteous life. I disassociate myself from any form of rebellion, any form of stubbornness, and any form of ignorance. I receive an influx of your Spirit. I connect back to your Spirit, and I retrieve back all that belongs to me. I have been set free, and so I am free indeed. No chains can bound me because I walk in obedience to Christ. As I walk in obedience, I receive the abundance of the blessings of my Father. In any way I have leaned to my ways of understanding, I hide in the Word of God in my life so that I will not sin against you. I repent, and I draw myself back to your Lordship. This is my heart cry for repentance.

Gaining
Spiritual immunity

Building and aligning are vital ingredients in this season for the unleashing of the awakened sons to colonize the ends of the earth!

DAY 22

I can do all things through Christ which strengtheneth me.
Philippians 4:13 (KJV)

The fact that they can lock you in your house with many restrictions does not mean you are down. Spiritually, we are not on lockdown! This is the time to prepare for launch. God is unleashing His own! The lockdown is not permanent, do not be misguided. This is the opportunity to take advantage of the time to align and prepare. The degree to which the kingdom must be expressed in you and the character to be revealed in you depends on your ability to align. This period is so important to awakening the true sons and for us to take our spiritual responsibility. Align yourself to spiritual immunity. We are mounting up our wings, arising so that we shine brighter and brighter unto a perfect day. Commit to the Lord whatever you do, and He will establish your plans.

This situation has enabled vast opportunities to connect and collect in this season. Be so allergic to a poverty mindset. Reject it completely. That mindset that tells you that you won't achieve anything is silenced in the name of Jesus Christ forever! You can still accomplish what you desire, your vision, purpose, goals, and destiny. You can empower your spirit man and your flesh to succeed beyond what many see as impossible. With God, all things are possible. Many are afraid to fail. But if you want to succeed, prepare to fail. Failure is a common experience that checks you and takes you to the path for success. If you ask people around you, they can testify that they have experienced failure. Their patience and consistency gave birth to success. If you have tried for the first time and it did not work, do not detach hope or be discouraged. Learn from it, pick yourself up, dust yourself, forget the pain and try again. Remember that procrastination is the key to frustration. Keep going; your preparation is not in vain. Always commit thy works unto the Lord, and your plans will succeed. Go for knowledge in this season so that you will not be frustrated. And knowing God's will for your life gives color to your vision.

Be those that are running with the vision of God and not like those burning with a passion. Be sensitive this season and connect to the season, so you know what to do, prepare. The grace has been released for the season. Be like the sons of Issachar who understood the times and knew what Israel ought to do. You are a son of God. Connect to the mind of God. We carry influence and express the kingdom in us that is to come. You are a citizen, an ambassador, and a son that is not bound by the system. You will prosper in all that you do. An important fact and truth that you may want to know is: You have a savings account in you to accomplish all that you desire that is in the will of God. Begin to build value now while you have no distractions. Your value is your virtue, the closeness and the authentic character of Christ. Set goals. Follow them up. Make sure they come to fruition because, without goals, there's no basis for being successful. Effectively develop the potentials in you. The effective use of your life, gifts, and resources to draw man to Jesus is called success and influence! Although success is not just the ability to show what you have achieved or accomplished. It is who you are becoming and growing into. It is not corporate and cannot be forced.
Succeed by all means. This does not mean anything and everything but follow legitimate processes. Yield to the Spirit, He will direct you and teach you. Yield to Him and begin to live a Spirit-filled life.

Here's something you should carry with you today: Don't

worry about your surroundings; keep building and yielding. Those significant efforts need to be seen. You have an unprecedented level and capacity to create an avenue for success.

Declaration

I am not locked down spiritually. I am unleashing the potential power I carry, and I walk in my sonship. The boundary lines have fallen for me in pleasant places, and I have a goodly heritage. I am entitled to an unprecedented level of success despite what I see because I walk not by sight but by faith. I am a citizen and an ambassador of the kingdom of heaven. I am not bound by what is going on; rather, I maximize this time and season for my growth. I receive spiritual immunity, and I develop my potentials. I key into the vast possibilities my government [kingdom] has to offer. I align myself to enjoy success. I am backed by God. I set goals, and I accomplish them. I can never be derailed not to fulfill my vision and my purpose. I succeed by all means through the help of the Holy Spirit. I follow the legitimate processes of spiritual growth in Jesus' Name.

Thank you, Father, because my words will be fulfilled, and I release my ministering spirits to bring every word I have spoken into manifestation.

How doors are handled

Our reception and treatment to the doors meant for us will determine our position, placement and advancement!

DAY 23

Be kindly affectioned one to another with brotherly love; in honor preferring one another;

Romans 12:10 (KJV)

People are doors; enter with care and handle with care! If you mess up, it is at your own risk. What am I driving at? Be careful how you treat people. No man is an island; we all need people for our next level and elevation. Be cautious about the aspect of the dimension of your reception. Our perception has aborted and closed the doors [people; destiny helpers] meant to nurture us and help us reach our proposed destination. We were quick to rule them out of our lives. We even escorted them out of the dealings of our lives. The spirit of discernment is very important for us not to miss our appointment. It is the highest faculty of perception.

Remember all things and every door worketh together for good to them that love Him and are called according to His purpose. Everybody knows somebody you do not know, and somebody can connect you to your destiny. God works through men. Men are facets of an extension and a manifestation of God. Do not be careless to parade yourself as an agent and a catalyst to shortchange your destiny. Avoid being too greedy for your safety. Be sensitive enough not to misuse the opportunities and possibilities around you. Some, their arrogant presumption of privilege has misguided them big time! Be wise. Use the eyes of your inner man to discern and not with the eye of the flesh. This is where fasting is important because it helps you subject your flesh and allow your spirit man to see beyond human capacity and discern in the Spirit.

May you walk through life with your heart and eyes open. The doors meant well, but the lack of transformation and untrained flesh went ahead of your spirit and took over matters into its care and deliberation. It is well; restoration is coming to you in Jesus' Name. Do not be in despair; God will arrange other doors to connect to you. You will not miss your appointment a second time. May our eyes of understanding be enlightened. Do not shoot yourself in your foot! Every door is important for your destination. Your doors call forth your provision. Do not let your character fight the doors God wants to open for you by making it difficult for those same doors to sow and be a channel and a fountain of blessings from above.

Many have left their doors with nothing for the imagination, nothing to compel them to help you because of your ignorance, lack of transformation and discernment. Until certain doors open for you, your running may be in vain. Your life may be a burden to you. God has delegated men, angels and the Holy Spirit to help us fulfill His purpose for our lives.

Here's something you should carry with you today: Doors are hallmarks of favor and destiny enablers. Be anointed for relationships with your doors!

Declaration

From today I repent from being careless with my doors. I receive discernment as a higher faculty of perception. I begin to perceive right. I call forth all the doors I have missed because of my carelessness in Jesus' Name to locate me. May I not stand against my destiny. With the Holy Spirit's help, I position myself to the vast opportunities and possibilities that will pave the way for my future to be colorful. I connect to the hallmarks of favor. May my eyes of understanding be enlightened. I judge not by the eyes of my flesh but by the eye of the Spirit. I receive transformation to be able to sustain relationships that God strategically constructs. I am anointed for relationships.

Generating savings

Savings are for our comfortability in life and they determine our wellbeing, thereby shielding us from experiencing hardships.

DAY 24

But what saith it? The word is nigh thee, even in thy mouth, and in thy heart: that is, the word of faith, which we preach;

Romans 10:8 (KJV)

You have a savings account in you!

You have the capacity and ability to withdraw what you need at any time. Yes, you can, and you have it. You may be wondering how it is possible to have an account in you that does not deal with monetary funds and value. We serve a God of wonders! But before anything else, the question you might want to ask yourself is whether if you are depositing the right savings and the best currency that will speak for you on your behalf and earn you interest in the long run. The Word of God in you and in your heart is the savings, faith is your currency, and the account is your spirit man. The application and engagement through your faith currency will earn you interest that will be evident and remain.

The Word stored in your heart crosschecked and confirmed with your spirit guarantees interest and made it inevitable not to accumulate. Bear in mind that it is only the savings [the Word] that have entered your account [inner man] that will guarantee safety and reliability! You can never be bankrupt; neither will your bank wind up or be bankrupt. The Word [savings] is alive and active; it is quick and powerful, sharper than any two-edged sword, piercing even to the dividing asunder of soul and spirit. Do not just store the savings in your account. Use them, do what the Word says! We live a life based on the Word, based on the Word in your spirit, and that has found expression to work through you. Activate your account now!

The Word will always give you access to attract all that you need. With your faith in the Word, you can frame anything you want, and you can speak forth things into existence. Do you want to live comfortably with an influx of plenty, a life overflowing with blessings and enjoy the bountifulness of your proceeds? Speak light. Then make sure your savings account is intact. Keep storing and depositing into your account, and eventually and at the end, it shall speak. You shall obtain a good report. Allow the Word to find expression. Make yourself a portal for the Word to sprout. Let your savings register in your account. Use your currency. That Word will become a lamp unto your feet and a light unto your path. It is a defense you will need in times of need. If your account is empty and there's a deficit, how will you survive in need? Stop crediting savings [the Word] that have not entered your account [spirit] to be effective and to bear results that are evident and undeniable. Trust your bank because you can have ease of withdrawal. Become that account that can never be empty!

Here's something you should carry with you today: Remember the Word is at your disposal. It is in your heart and your mouth. Make contact with your spirit, use it, and recharge your account for your good and future purposes

Declaration

I have the capacity and ability for the Word of God to be fruitful in my life because I withdraw from my spirit and put the Word to use. The Word in me is profiting my soul. I engage my faith currency in speaking what I want to see and experience God's blessings in my life. My account is ever loaded with the Word that giveth life and light to my spirit. Again, from today, I register, recharge, and activate my account to harvest my proceeds. I receive interest in every Word at work in me, and I enjoy my harvest's bountifulness. I engage my faith, and I enjoy the benefits of my faith from today onwards!

Thank you, Lord, for giving me savings that are always reliable and provide food to my soul.

Developing impact for insight

Walking with God circumspectly creates a level of purity in the Spirit that commands fruits that remain and fruits that echo to eternity!

DAY 25

For it is God which worketh in you both to will and do of his good pleasure.

Philippians 2:13 (KJV)

Life is how much you impact people's lives. It is how much you also maintain the impact that matters. It goes beyond just how much and what you can attain. Men of honor and impact are those that believe they were born for a season. Do you want to be impactful in this generation? Then gain insight into the Word of God. Impact is a product of insight! Looking at success, you discover that it has more to do with how much impact you have made and who you are becoming. Only shallow-minded people believe only in what they have achieved or accomplished individually for themselves. They see success through the lens of self. It is more blessed to give than to receive. Never underestimate the depth of impact you can render. You are loaded, don't be too quick to think that you are empty or dismiss the truth of what you carry inside of you that must find expression.

Life is dimensional. There are graces you carry that others need to be partakers of! God downloaded Himself in you to impact your generation. Your Father of light did not create light [you] not to be impactful. He created light to shine and give direction, to give life meaning to many. Because right now and at this moment, you cannot draw certain dimensions higher than you does not mean you have nothing to offer. No! Change that perception. People are waiting for that which you carry. There's always room for growth. Your life is for a purpose, and in that purpose lies your impact, and your purpose comes with power!

The effective use of your life, gifts and resources to draw men to the kingdom is called impact. Keep investing in the kingdom; influence and impact are inevitable. Remember, the impact is not proving a point; it reveals the dimensions of His presence, nature and character in you. Reinforce yourself in the Spirit. Graduate from the life of the majority. You are born to make an impact, for it is God who worketh in you both to will and to do of His pleasure. Begin to start impacting your environment to allow divinity to find expression in you. Exercise the Word inside you. It is meant to impact you and your generation. Let your light so shine before men, and those that see your good works will glorify the Father. Don't worry; keep building, impact. By your fruits, we shall know you!

Relevance and impact are a level of purity in the Spirit when you have walked with God circumspectly, for He makes His angels spirits and His ministers flames of fire! Kindle the passion for genuine kingdom impact for you to see the fruits that remain and reiterate to eternity. When you function on this kind of energy, you become accurate with God. The price of all of God is all of you! You want to be relevant and be impactful? You want your name not to just vanish on the face of the earth? Well, what then is the level of your sacrifice? Through yielding, one can attain growth by the responsibilities and level of sacrifice rendered in both the spiritual and the physical realm. Your sacrifice for the kingdom is a strategy of heaven for taking over altars. This will, however, determine your relevance at that level. Those that walk in the Spirit never run from being ambassadors and representatives of the kingdom mandate. Do you know you can play your life like chess by your relevance, and you can experience vast realms of possibilities that will arrange themselves for your sake, child of God!? Make an impact and become a source and a voice. Make an impact, and attain your respect!

Here's something you should carry with you today: Your impact is your testimony and a testament of the dimension of God that has found a portal for expression. You are the light of the world and a city set upon a hill that cannot be hidden.

Declaration

I am born to make and maintain my impact. I am loaded, and I carry graces for my generation. I effectively use my life, gifts and resources to draw people to the kingdom. My life is a testimony. My life is a pointer to the glory and grace of God. I will begin to develop myself and work on myself to draw influence. I am the light of this world, the salt of this earth and I give my generation flavour. I am able; I am capable, I am distinguishable, I am fashionable, I am knowledgeable, I am accountable, I am influenceable, I am unstoppable, and I am valuable to the kingdom. I am in the generation of impact!

Soul wining mandate

It is the duty and a priority for born again believers to actively contribute to the kingdom advancement; our manual is to be wise in winning souls back to the kingdom.

DAY 26

The fruit of the righteous is a tree of life; and he that winneth a soul is wise.

Proverbs 11:30 (KJV)

The heart for soul winning…
A mandate for all believers…

Wisdom nugget: Our mandate as believers is to establish the Lordship of Jesus Christ in the hearts of men. It is a priority in the kingdom! As believers who are born of God and carry the Father's DNA, we are branches of the vine. And it is our sole duty and purpose to bear fruits that are evident, fruits that remain. People only know how to pray for needs like money, food, relationships, and selfish desires like their enemies' death before their time. Yet, we do not know how to pray and win souls for the kingdom. We are no longer passionate to win souls. We have the life of God. We are the tree of life that makes it possible for discipleship and sonship lineage to expand exponentially. If your life, prosperity, preaching and service does not win souls, it is a waste to God!

Let us take our rightful places and make up our minds to use our gifts, skills, resources, beauty, influence, voice to point men to Jesus and draw them to Him. Jesus needs to be revealed above systems and structures through our dominion. *"How then shall they call on him in whom they have not believed? and how shall they believe in him of whom they have not heard? and how shall they hear without a preacher? And how shall they preach, except they be sent? as it is writ-*

ten, How beautiful are the feet of them that preach the gospel of peace, and bring glad tidings of good things!" Romans 10:14-15 (KJV). Blessed are they that do His commandments; that they may have the right to the tree of life, and may enter in through the gates into the city.

We are like a tree planted by the rivers of water, meaning to say we always bring forth fruits in and out of season because we are the righteousness of God in Him. We carry the Spirit and the life of God for healing to the nations. Be an evangelist, a physician and a teacher of the spread of the good news. It is that time for harvesting souls for the kingdom. The harvest is plenty! Be relevant in the program of God. Be wise if you will… Wisdom just doesn't function in the brain; it shows when you act and when you talk! So, go ye into the world and preach the gospel. Prove the Word in your life, put God to the test and see Him perform. Wisdom is a tree of life to those who lay hold of it. And if you love your soul, get wisdom, win souls, and contribute to their lifting! Do not be found not bearing fruits because you will be taken away and cast into the fire for lack of fruits. The Mimshack anointing is upon you; the grace is upon you. Be a contributor to the spiritual life, health and healing of lost souls by bringing them to the knowledge of God and the obedience to Christ. Be among those whose fruits will be seen [by their fruits, you shall know them]. The more you change other people's lives, the greater the glory of your own life! Be a soul hunter; be a fisher of man!

Part of a believer's manual is to contribute actively to the kingdom's advancement and allow God to find expression of His purpose through you. Never for one day unsubscribe to the mandate of winning souls. Wherever you are, be it at work, school anywhere in the world, do not trivialize the efficacy of soul winning. Do you want to stay winning? Win souls and cause heaven to always answer to your call. This is a principle that sources blessings. Win souls and triumph into unimaginable blessings! Make it a duty and a lifestyle to at least win somebody to the kingdom. Have a name connected to you, that you won to Christ.

Be part of others' success story when they are found and when they return to the kingdom. How useful are you to the kingdom? Be actively useful. If you haven't seen the need to be an evangelist, you can start now. It is never too late. It is better late than never. I know you can do it! I trust you will. The Lord is your strength. Did you know that the easiest way to evangelize to somebody is to use your own story? Many may not believe until they see proof. Show them the testament of your life. You might think you are not worded, do not worry at all; there are many alternatives you can use based on your confidence. Remember, for God to come, it is dependent on us to spread the gospel to the ends of the earth. Your usefulness in the kingdom determines protection and provision. It is not just going to church because that is a testimonial portion of your service; it is about your usefulness to God's plan and His church. When you save young people out there, be guaranteed that you have saved a generation! Create heritage for the next generation; I beg you, brethren.

Here's something you should carry with you today: Your good act of service and a higher calling is winning souls [changing lives]. And they that be wise shall shine as the brightness of the firmament; they shall turn many to righteousness as the stars for ever and ever.

Declaration

Father, I believe in my mandate to remain effective in soul winning. Let my passion for souls keep burning by the day. From today I become a contributor to the spiritual life, health and healing of lost souls. I establish your Lordship on this earth in the hearts of man. I bare fruits that remain in the kingdom and for the kingdom. I develop a passion for winning souls. I take my rightful place, and I make up my mind to use my gifts, skills, resources, beauty, influence and voice to point men to Jesus and draw them to Him. I reveal Jesus above systems and structures through my dominion mandate. Thank you for making your grace available and accessible for me as I embark on the harvest. I am wise, and I am filled with the wisdom of God in the Name of Jesus.

Thank you, Father, for empowering me and sending me into the world.

Power
under control

*Submission is important
to be led effectively in the kingdom.*

DAY 27

Submit yourselves therefore to God. Resist the devil, and he will flee from you.

James 4:7 (KJV)

Some say submission is demeaning yourself. But I say submission is power under control! The power of me and I over the power of the Lordship of Jesus Christ. If the world has colonized you, come back to God and subject yourself to the Word. Stop submitting to social media and other worldly sources. Are you submitted to God? Submit to the sovereignty of the kingdom jurisdiction and its legislation. Submit to the mission of God; this is submission. There's a need for submission for God's vision to come to fruition. This is for your profiting and increase. Are you willing to sacrifice your own opinion for what God says over your life? Submission is a form of humility, and refusing to submit to God leads to a life of defeat and pain. God resists the proud, and He gives more grace to the humble. Submission must be genuine for you to enjoy the grace. Submission profits the submitter, not the one being submitted to! Remember, you are never doing a favor to the one you are submitting to and, in this case, to God.

Do you know that God honors you? Why not reciprocate. You cannot honor a leader without the leader honoring you. Deposit yourself. Waste yourself in submission to God and see how it pays off. It might be costly, but it is for your convenience. Submission is deeper than doctrine. We need to come to a point where we mirror and submit ourselves just as that submission of a husband and a wife. We are the wife and Christ, is our husband. We need to submit to fulfill our destinies. Although there's a price you pay to stay submitted to God constantly, the result is overwhelming and unmatched. Submission is a system of rising. Do you want to grow in the kingdom? The key is to submit. Submit yourselves, therefore, to God. Resist the devil, and he will flee from you.

Your act of submission is reverence to God. It is a testimony of leap that we depend on God and not on our youthfulness. It is a scriptural pattern to submit for things to flow to you. Remember, a mindset on the flesh is hostile to God and does not submit to God's authority. Submission gives you access to the realm of the Spirit. It is a system of acknowledgement. The benefits that come with submission is protection, provision and promotion. Submission is humility and reverence to a higher authority.

Submission attracts favor, and it comes with power. Through submission, you become a facilitator of the kingdom principles. Submission to the kingdom's government and the Holy Spirit is death to the yearnings of the soul! Submit to the leadership of His Spirit and see yourself become powerful while in submission. The road to attaining power is when you trade your pride with obedience, yieldedness, a broken spirit and a contrite heart, trading your self-sufficiency with obedience. When you recognize your shortcomings and imperfections, aside from God's help, grace, and mercy, you are pruned when you surrender to God. The attestation of your submission allows Him to find expression in you and through you. It is proof of humility and starving your pride from anything that causes you to grow. Submission is making yourself become a vessel unto honor. It is a state of exchanging your weaknesses with the covering and the strength of God. It is proof of your dependency on the high calling of God.

Here's something you should carry with you today: Your ability to submit to God opens up infinite possibilities.

Declaration

Today I submit to the mission of the Lordship of Jesus Christ. I subject myself to the power and vision of God. I honor and yield myself to the leadership of my Father. I humble myself in humility to the jurisdiction of God. I align genuinely with you, Father, by faith. As I submit to your Lordship, I know a compendium of infinite possibilities will be opened before me. I am a benefactor of the grace, glory, anointing and the power of Yeshua. I key into this system of acknowledgement and rising in the Name of Jesus Christ. My mind can never be hostile to God because today, I submit to God's authority. I gain access to the realms of the Spirit. I believe my submission is for my protection, provision and promotion. The veil for vast possibilities of God is opened before me in Jesus' Name.

Prayer

*Prayer gives you access to navigate in all
spheres of life and it allows you to engage
God, angels, principalities and atmospheres!*

DAY 28

… that men ought always to pray, and not faint;
Luke 18:1 (KJV)

Likewise the Spirit also helpeth our infirmities: for we know not what we should pray for as we ought: but the Spirit itself maketh intercession for us with groanings which cannot be uttered.
Romans 8:26 (KJV)

Confess your faults one to another, and pray one for another, that ye may be healed. The effectual fervent prayer of a righteous man availeth much.
James 5:16 (KJV)

Do you want to be exceptional and to dwell in vast realms of possibilities? The answer is simple, prayer! Yes, you read right, prayer. Prayer is hard, but it is the only way. Did you know that the primary assignment of prayer is to change you and change your needs? Well, prayer is a system of transferring and converting spiritual realities into the physical realm. It is a system of kingdom legislation that we need to fathom as believers. The only person delaying your breakthrough, prosperity, direction and next level is you because of not keying into the system of prayer. It should become a lifestyle and not a burden or an activity we resort to when we are only stranded and out of options. And when we engage in prayer, we allow the Spirit to search the mind of the Father.

Men always ought to pray and not to faint. The exemption that is permitted is for anything or those that are not men. You are a man. When there's a man to pray, there's a God to answer. Prayer is your charger so that you avert from fainting. Grow your way through prayer. Maintain the glow of the Spirit. And if you don't pray, you detach the spiritual flavors that come with it. Never trust the result you see if you haven't prayed. Until you have secured in prayer, then you can be guaranteed of the fruits. You sustain your prayer life through fasting and by the Word of God. Pray!

Prayer gives access to power; it directs, corrects, illuminates, restores and distinguishes you from being ordinary. Zoom into prayer to keep discovering Him. Seek Him in prayer, and you will find Him. Most of the time, we are frustrated in prayer because we pray amiss; we pray outside God's will. And how then will you pray the Word when you do not know His will and when you do not know His Word? We have confidence in Him that when we ask anything according to His will, He hears us. The place of the Word is important because we pray the Word and not problems. Put on your priestly regalia. We have been made kings and priests unto God. Utilize your priesthood office.

Begin to journey away from your flesh and join with God. An altar of prayer is an altar of power. Your prayerlessness can coordinate possibilities you desire in the Spirit and give you access to select all you need and want to manifest. You might say you don't know how to pray, but it is the Spirit that helps us and makes intercessions for us with groanings that cannot be uttered. Just open your mouth, and He will fill it.

Prayerlessness is a sign of pride, and you trivialize the relevance of God in your life. Are you humble? Then pray! Prayer is proof of your humility. Prayer has to do with your repentant heart and a broken Spirit. Engage your faith currency in the place of prayer and begin to enjoy the benefits of your faith. You shall call upon Him, and you shall go and pray unto Him, and He will hearken unto you. Understand the jurisdiction of prayer so that when you pray, you know you are interacting with God. Labor to enter into this Truth! Prayer clothes us with the strength of God, and when we pray, we exchange our weakness with His strength. And with prayer, you live above the elements of this world. It's time to pray, son of God. Prayerful people are presence-full people. You will always sense God in them because they are continuously filled with the Spirit of God.

You can navigate your spiritual territory through prayer, did you know? And again, did you know that we are all equal in salvation but different in the kingdom? Your prayerfulness separates you from the ordinary flock. Develop the hunger for prayer. You can start small and grow little by little with the Holy Spirit's help, which helps us pray. And when you develop stamina and weight in the Spirit, then you will exhibit the nature of God. Prayer causes your countenance to change because of the intimacy developed over time through your consistency. You will become a host of the very presence of God, and you will always be full. Allow God to go on a honeymoon with you. Allow Him to teach you something unique. He is seducing you to come to His presence and dwell there. Give in! Submit! You are His bride! The level of intimacy with God makes you immune to the devious ways of the enemy. Many are still complete novices to God's things and yet experts in this world's sophisticated systems and technology. But God is saying, "Come up, hither!"

Use your energy to pray and to seek God, for it is far better than to misuse your power. For energy not used or accounted for properly in the kingdom qualifies for disaster! Prayer is when you engage God, angels [ministering spirits] and sometimes principalities and atmospheres. The testimony of your secret place is greater than the testimony of speaking on the altar. Prayer needs time and submission for it to work. Know for a fact that there's a rejection of prayer that is in your soul. Stay in the secret place. Consistency tests character. When the character is built, your virtue, trust, opportunity, and destiny speaks where your voice cannot speak! Let it not just be about the gifts without the backing of prayer because gifts are without repentance. That is why they are called gifts; they cannot be claimed back. Remember, so great a cloud of witnesses surrounds us. Be willing to improve on your prayer life and see things turnaround for your good.

Here's something you should carry with you today: Prayer begins with your consciousness and your yieldedness to the Spirit. It is a vital ingredient in our lives. It is a testimony of your worship and a testament of proof that we depend on God. Build capacity in the place of prayer, knowing it is not a visitation but a habitation.

Declaration

From today I develop consciousness, and I yield myself to the Spirit. I set my altar of prayer on fire, and I maintain the glow of the Spirit. May I not eject this ingredient, the fragrance and flavor in my life. I build capacity in my secret place. Prayer will become my lifestyle and the testimony of my worship. My total dependency is on you, Lord. Holy Spirit teach me to pray. I will open my mouth, and I know you will fill it. I receive the strength to pray in the Name of Jesus. I humble myself before your throne of grace, Lord, and I consecrate myself in faith through prayer, for I know that my prayer life will never remain the same after today. May I encounter you in my place of prayer. From today I understand the jurisdiction of prayer because I know that this is my ticket to being elevated above the elements of this world. I distinguish myself from being ordinary, and I wear on my priestly regalia in the Name of Jesus.

The protocol
of His presence

*The presence of God is a must that should
always be carried by sons of God because we
are hosts of His divinity!*

DAY 29

And he said, My presence shall go with thee, and I will give thee rest. And he said unto him, If thy presence go not with me, carry us not up hence.

Exodus 33:14-15 (KJV)

When you learn His presence, you will see how cheap the devil is! You become untouchable and an off zone to the devil. The devil will not do what he wants to you. His presence cannot be faked. It is not just a theory; His presence is the secret of power. The presence of God is a vehicle, a transportation channel for those who are connected to Him. There is a pattern you need to adhere to enjoy His presence. We need to receive a new layer of the baptism of His presence. This is a new season; we must all carry the presence. New seasons demands new things, and we must endeavor to culminate His presence. Let your operating system of being a Christian and your walk be a life deposited with the presence of God in your spirit. Many carry oil, but not many carry His presence. When you are in sync with God, His presence is inevitable.

Keep yourself in balance with the presence of God. In Him, we have boldness and access with confidence by the faith of Him. Where can you go from His Spirit, and where can you flee from His presence? For in Him we live, we move and have our being. Let us now come before His presence with thanksgiving; in His presence, there's fullness of joy, peace, rest, direction, anointing and assurance of His manifested dimensions. In these difficult times, His presence is vital to life's journey, progress and destiny. Whatever we might be going through just needs the invasion, interference and introduction of the presence of God. His presence breaks protocol in the physical realm. There's a price to pay for His presence. Let us, therefore, maintain consecration and sanctification.

Learn to connect to the potential presence of God; His Spirit dwells in you. Let your heart stay in Him so that you benefit from the availability and profitability of His presence. His presence is no respecter of persons, develop a broken spirit and a contrite heart. The deeper your humility, the greater the presence! *"For thus saith the high and lofty One that inhabiteth eternity, whose name is Holy; I dwell in the high and holy place, with him also that is of a contrite and humble spirit, to revive the spirit of the humble, and to revive the heart of the contrite ones." Isaiah57:15 (KJV).* Disengage from your flesh and stay connected to His Spirit to maintain His presence. Be quickened in the spirit and receive consciousness. Practice the presence of God.

There are things in your life, areas in your life you may never see outside of His presence. And there are things that you are struggling with that will be uplifted from you and nullified by the consciousness of His presence. Draw near to Him, and He will draw near to you. God wants to make known His plan, agenda and program to you. Let us align ourselves to Him to be benefactors and beneficiaries of His very presence. People should feel the presence when they see you and when they come in contact with your person. The idea of the presence is for you to dwell there! Alignment will cause us to experience the presence of God. God is calling every one of us into His presence. He wants to shift things in our lives so that we can walk fully in His presence. He wants to give us access, reveal to you things you do not know. There's a place He is calling you into; that is the secret place. A prayerful person is a presence-full person…!

All that God is, is His presence. God's presence is the nature, character, His heart and manifestation. He is the power, grace, mercy and love. Let us, therefore, now come to the dimension of understanding the protocol of the secret place to enjoy the presence of God.

The very presence of God is His protocol! Hunger for His presence. Let it be an atmosphere that resonates within you. Unfortunately, we are in a century where the church glories in crowds than stature. Desire the presence and brokenness. The Lord is nigh unto them that are of a broken heart and a contrite spirit. He never despises when you come to Him with all sincerity of heart. When you go to Him with this, His presence is inevitable. He will not withhold from you from experiencing Him. When you exchange your weakness with His strength, you will become a host for His dear presence. You see, power can be faked, but one thing that can never be faked or acted upon is His presence. His presence is for assistance. Presence is not automatic because you are a believer, a man of God, a woman of God, or if you preach so well. No. It is a state of a healthy secret place. Cultivate it. His Spirit is always with you. Now work on manifesting His presence. It is an experience you will forever be grateful for and enjoy. May God take us deeper in Jesus Name! Become the fire from today and become untouchable and unstoppable because it is your essence that is communicated through His presence in the Spirit. We need a new baptism of His fire.

Here's something you should carry with you today: God wants us to enjoy the fullness of His presence in our spiritual walk with Him. Let us develop and cultivate the presence of God in our lives and affairs to see the acceleration of God's presence is made manifest.

Declaration

I cultivate the presence of God because I walk in the realm of His abiding presence. This is my new season to experience His presence like never before. I receive a fresh baptism of His presence. Lord, any trace of arrogance or pride that will deprive me of your presence, take it away, Lord. Help me to maintain consecration and sanctification. May I be of an authentic contrite heart and of a broken spirit for your presence to abide in me forever. May I be always in check with your presence in my dealings with you, Lord. As I go all the way with God, I will begin to enjoy the benefits of the availability and profitability of His presence. May I be prayerful to be presence-full. Quicken my spirit so that I receive the consciousness of your presence in my life in the Name of Jesus. And may I not be seen operating outside of the presence of God from today in my life. Thank you, Father, for calling me into your presence.

The Holy Spirit: Our lover

The Holy Spirit is for an extra-ordinary life;
He is our teacher, leader, helper, advocate
and our guide. He is for our profiting and His
involvement in our lives goes a long way.

DAY 30

But if the Spirit of him that raised up Jesus from the dead dwell in you, he that raised up Christ from the dead shall also quicken your mortal bodies by his Spirit that dwelleth in you.

Romans 8:11 (KJV)

For as many as are led by the Spirit of God, they are the sons of God.

Romans 8:14 (KJV)

The most neglected person in our lives who so happen to be the most important person and part of our Christian living is the person of the Holy Spirit. He is the One sent by God here on earth. He has the mandate to lead us into all truth. The Holy Spirit is our spiritual housekeeper. He dwells in us and desires our house [body] to be spiritually kept, minded, and always walk in the Spirit. You might be asking who He is and what is His importance to your lives, and if you can live a life without Him. Well, the Holy Spirit is a personality. He has feelings, and He can be grieved. He speaks. He touches; He can be felt. He is about the business of our Father, the manifestation of the miraculous, the supernatural. He is the manifestation of the presence of God. He is intelligent, full of the wisdom of God, and He is the power of God!

If you desire a life full of advantages, the supernatural and for Him to help you pray, then you need Him big time in your life. And if we must understand the Holy Spirit, we must understand the kingdom. He wants to rule, to dominate our lives and to take over and lead the affairs of our lives. We must come to a point where we acknowledge and recognize the seniority of the Spirit's involvement and submit our flesh for Him to quicken us. Do you want to subject yourself to Him? Do you want Him to permeate everlasting joy? Then you must allow Him. He is the power of God acting on the Word. The dispensation of the Spirit is to be our comforter, our advocate. He is our helper who helps us interpret the Word, serve adequately, effectively, and live a Spirit life. Let us, therefore, walk in the Spirit so as not to fulfil the lust of the flesh.

The same Spirit that was hovering over the face of the earth and the waters is the same Spirit that dwells in us. We have the creative Spirit in us. Did you know that everything we will ever receive comes from the Spirit? Therefore, let us not walk after the flesh but after the Spirit because to be spiritually minded is life and peace, but to be carnally minded is death. In these last days, God will pour out His Spirit upon all flesh, and we shall prophesy, see visions and dream dreams. It is easier to know the Will of the Father if we allow the Holy Spirit to direct us.

The Holy Spirit wants to be your friend; let us not neglect Him for anything. The degree to which your body can be yielded to the Spirit will be seen by how much God will be made manifest in you and through you. Be Spiritually conscious. The Spirit wants to equip us to empower the World. Those that His Spirit leads are the sons of God, and we have received the Spirit of adoption whereby we cry Abba Father. The Holy Spirit is a vital part of every single believer's life. Remember, it is not by might nor by power, but it is by His Spirit. He teaches us all things, and brings all things to our remembrance and reveals to us deep things that are of the Spirit. Fellowship with Him from today and see your life be transformed. Those that know the Spirit of God will know the mind of God. The Holy Spirit is a communicator of spiritual intelligence and a giver of supernatural ability. He is the seal of our salvation. And we also have been made able ministers of the Spirit and that same Spirit giveth life.

If you want an ordinary life, then you don't need the Holy Spirit! The Holy Spirit is not meant for ordinary living. He makes you exceptional. He makes your life supernatural and extraordinary. But you have to learn to function in the realm with the involvement of His Spirit. The Holy Spirit is the garment that shields us from the system of the world. The key to success is the involvement of the Holy Spirit. Submit to the government of the Holy Spirit if you want a creative life. He is a must. Make Him your companion. He will help us with a spectrum of possibilities. The Spirit of God is co-equal with the Godhead, God the Father and God the Son. There are the trinity. He is all-powerful, and He is present everywhere at the same time. You cannot get away from Him; you can only be just unconscious of Him. Nothing is hidden from Him. He is a liberator. He makes us alive because we are all dead men walking that need the Holy Spirit to be made alive! He baptizes us into the body of Christ. He empowers us for service, and we have received power because we have received Him. Our Helper is the producer of the fruits of the Spirit. Our Comforter is the attribute of Jesus Himself. And you cannot be alive as a Christian by yourself; you will be signing for disaster. You surely need Him.

Here's something you should carry with you today: We have received the Spirit of God and not the spirit of this world that we might know the things that are freely given to us of God. Fellowship with His Spirit and involve Him in all that you do.

Declaration

I will no longer neglect the Spirit of God in my life. His involvement in my life is for my profiting, for my teaching, for my leading, for me to know the Truth and to live a Spirit life! Abba Father, I thank you for giving me the Spirit of adoption. Help me, Lord, not to grieve the person of the Holy Spirit in all that I do. And may I always include Him in my dealings. I know it is not by might nor by power, but it is by your Spirit. I receive your Spirit afresh; I receive the baptism of the Holy Spirit, and I align myself to be a partaker of the miraculous, the supernatural and the manifestation of the presence of God. I am an able minister of the Spirit, and I have not received the spirit of this world but the Spirit of God to know the things freely given to me of God. From today, I develop Spiritual consciousness. Equip me and empower me, Holy Spirit, for the work I ought to do in this world. May I walk with you to experience the fruits of the Spirit. Be my friend Holy Spirit. Be my light. Be my guide. Be my way. Be my will and Be my teacher.

Identity

Your identity in Christ shields you from the manipulation and being made vulnerable and targeted by the enemy!

DAY 31

But as many as received him, to them gave he power to become the sons of God, even to them that believed on his name:

John 1:12 (KJV)

Finishing strong…
Sons of God is not a title but an empowerment!

Doubt your doubts before you doubt God of your identity and empowerment! You are the ecclesia. God chose you and ordained you. You were crucified with Him, and you are in partnership with God. Unmask your true self! Allow your true height to show. Stop wearing the false identity. It is exhausting… Your future is looking for you, but not this version of you. You are a God, the replica and an extension of God. As He is, so are you in this world. Your significance is tied to who you are. If you don't know yourself, you will die a nonentity! The revelation of who you are is key to your inheritance and your manifestation. There are things in you, businesses, ideas, visions, ministries, relationships and many other things that are just waiting for you to realize and start walking in them.

Unmask yourself!!! We have a propensity of not portraying who we are. Can you imagine; God made you in His image, and it is only you who He made in His image. Not even the angels were created in His image. You are a co-creator. If only you knew that everything you desire and everything you want to become or need could be drawn from within the bowls of your spirit. God has risen in your favor; victory is yours.

Success only answers to identity and not through the lens of ignorance. Exercise your willpower. You see, you have the power to frame, the ability to create and the capacity to design and bring forth greatness in you. The fullness of the Godhead dwells in you. And out of our belly shall flow rivers of living waters. Do you believe it? God created the worlds with His Spirit, and He gave you the same Spirit, and by giving you the same Spirit, He gave you the same ability.

Taste and see that the Lord is indeed good, and He has gifted you beyond what you can comprehend. Taste and see, God wants to do exceedingly abundantly above all that you can ask or think, according to the power at work in you. Discover the hidden gifts within you and secure authority and power you carry that has been dormant. Enough is enough; the time to be powerless is over! Reignite, light up. God gave Himself to you; He is your reward! Therefore, be confident in who you are, in your identity so that you will not face intimidation by the enemy. Your knowledge will eliminate every embargo supplied by ignorance. The reason you cannot walk in power is that you do not know you are. You are a carrier of the very power of God. Invest in yourself by acquiring knowledge, and you will do exploits. The more of God you know, the more like Him you become. The revelation of your identity is very important if you want to be victorious. God said, "Let there be light," and there was you [put your name]. You are a city set upon a hill that cannot be hidden. Meditate on the Word, so you capture your identity in the Word.

Here's something you should carry with you today: The greatest joy and asset you can give yourself as a believer, a son of God, is to know who you are and when you discover this truth about your identity, you take dominion!

Declaration

I am a son of God, not just by title; I am an empowered son of God. I have been crucified with Him, and I partner with God. Today I walk in the revelation knowledge of who I am. I walk in my divine assignment. I am a God, the exact imprint of His extension and nature; therefore, I can never be a nonentity. I am filled with His Spirit, and I walk in my inheritance and the power of God. I stand at my true height. I have dominion, and I am a co-creator with my Father. I no longer walk in ignorance of my identity. I know who I am in Christ, Jesus.

Conclusion

Our lives need to be preserved as long as we remain in God and on this earth because our flesh is not trained on proper management and maintenance of the Spirit. And this is why we need to always be in the Spirit so that the Spirit teaches our flesh. The Spirit's seniority should always be recognized, and there must be a continuous submission of our flesh to the Spirit. We must continually cultivate and culminate the presence of God in our lives to come to a dimension of the knowledge of God and His Word for ourselves. We have been born of the Spirit; therefore, we must remain and walk in the Spirit at all times for us not to be powerless, irrelevant and not valuable in this world. Our lives should be a testimony and a testament to our dependency on God alone. We need to draw closer to Him so that He draws Himself closer to us and for us to enjoy His presence and His manifestation. We have been given the very life of God [zoweh] through His Spirit. In these difficult times, we need to be prayerful to know what we ought to do. A Spirit life is a lifestyle we must cultivate and draw from the Spirit through the Word of God. We lack knowledge not because there's no knowledge, but we lack knowledge because we have rejected knowledge. We don't lack God but knowledge. Because we have been given the capacity to accommodate multiple spirits [Holy Spirit, spirit of this world, evil spirits and many other spirits], this is why we need to know our identity in Christ [being hidden with Christ in God]. Keep investing in knowledge to understand and function in your identity fully. You are a God!!!

Congratulations!!!

You did it! You have managed to finish this journey to living a Spirit life! I hope you have learnt so much. I hope you are implementing and practicing living righteously because we have all been made the righteousness of God in Christ Jesus. I am so pleased to see you accomplish great and mighty things through His Spirit. Know that your investment was not in vain; He will reward you for your diligence. His Lordship will see you through. May His face shine upon you, and may you enjoy the benefits of your faith and your yieldedness to His Spirit. I love you with the love of God, and may the grace of our Lord Jesus Christ be with you all. Amen

For all your testimonies and reviews, please email us at the email address below. Those who genuinely made the prayer to be saved can email us their details: your name, number and the country you are from. We want to congratulate you and be responsible for your growth in the kingdom, and see you manifest into your true height!

chroniclesofthenewmove@gmail.com

Visit our website for more information
www.awakeningthesons.com

About the Author

Olga Matsanura is a holder of an International Law degree and mastering in Social Work. She is an upcoming new generation writer who has an intense hunger to see young people grow in their full height and capacity. Her passion and heart cry; is focused on spreading the good news unapologetically to the world to eliminate a carnally minded mentality and to cultivate an appetite for the Word of God. She is a student and a product of In-Spirited Writers Training School. She strongly believes in unlocking believers' minds to manifest, navigate, and get hold of their spiritual territories in a simplified manner that many may accept. The author aims to reach many and see transformation in believers' lives across the globe.